Praise for *A Footnote to Freedom*

A touching and human view of a part of our history that has long been ignored in Canada. *A Footnote to Freedom* reminds us that behind historical events lie the families and people that have survived them and continued to build lives for themselves despite hardship and struggle.

— **CAITLIN BAILEY**, executive director, Vimy Foundation

This is a book about a battalion, a community, a country, and a family; it is also a book about silence — how it can hide, suppress, and wound — and how that silence can be engaged with love. *A Footnote to Freedom* shows that speaking about the past can be an act of care, both for our ancestors and for ourselves.

— **AARON CURTIS**, lead educator, Valour Canada

A wonderfully told story of justice and recognition. This book should be compulsory reading as we continue to fill in the missing gaps in our national narrative, especially the untold stories of Black Canadians, their sacrifices, and their gallantry [in] making Canada what it is today.

— **CECIL FOSTER**, author of *They Call Me George: The Untold Story of Black Train Porters and the Birth of Modern Canada*

A complex and nuanced story about the impact centuries of racism and discrimination can have — not only on a soldier in Canada's segregated Black Battalion but also on the generations of family that followed. By having painful and difficult conversations with his father, Lance B. Dixon brings history to life in vivid detail while exercising ghosts from the past, leaving behind empathy, compassion, and a deep understanding of the power of forgiveness.

— **KEVIN O'KEEFE**, former producer of *W5*

The Black Battalion is one of Canada's lesser-known military stories. Still, to truly understand its importance, we need to look at the lives and wartime experiences of the men who served and the families who stood by them. Our national history is made up of many individual stories, with ordinary people achieving extraordinary things and remarkable individuals showing quiet strength. By sharing the poignant story of his grandfather through his father's recollections, Lance B. Dixon not only revives cherished family memories but also highlights a crucial chapter in our understanding of the Black Battalion and the broader narrative of our nation's history.

— **DOUGLAS G. RUCK, K.C.**

In *A Footnote to Freedom*, Lance B. Dixon proves himself a gifted storyteller, transporting the reader back in time by weaving fabrics of poetic and imaginative descriptions of his family's history with eloquent revelations about a unique part of Canadian history. The author paints colourful images of early African Canadian settlements in Nova Scotia and New Brunswick with intriguing characters who help mould a compelling story. Lance takes us on a captivating and emotional journey of self-discovery and reveals the importance of learning one's family roots. The book is a personal and touching tribute to his father and to George Dixon, his grandfather, who served in Canada's all-Black Battalion during the First World War.

— **ANTHONY SHERWOOD**, award-winning Canadian actor, filmmaker, and activist

In this stunningly woven narrative, Dixon takes readers on an important journey, not only to understand his own family history but also to hold a mirror to a nation's racism, both past and present. With careful craft and powerful prose, Dixon captivates readers and simultaneously shows us how prejudice impacts an organization, a country, and one particular family, ensuring the six hundred Black soldiers of No. 2 Construction Battalion are rightfully canonized in Canada's military history. This story of resilience, bravery, and determination is a whopper of a debut that belongs on the bookshelves of every civil rights activist and historian.

— **DR. KELLY S. THOMPSON**, retired military officer and national bestselling author of *Girls Need Not Apply: Field Notes from the Forces*

A FOOTNOTE TO FREEDOM

A FOOTNOTE TO FREEDOM

RECLAIMING THE LIFE AND LEGACY OF A BLACK BATTALION SOLDIER

LANCE B. DIXON

DUNDURN PRESS

Publisher and acquiring editor: Meghan Macdonald | Editor: Carrie Gleason
Cover designer: Laura Boyle
Cover images: (*top*) No. 2 Construction Battalion by H.C. Dodge; (*bottom*) Jennifer Dow

Library and Archives Canada Cataloguing in Publication

Title: A footnote to freedom : reclaiming the life and legacy of a Black battalion soldier / Lance B. Dixon.
Names: Dixon, Lance B., author.
Identifiers: Canadiana (print) 20250317915 | Canadiana (ebook) 20250318156 | ISBN 9781459756977 (softcover) | ISBN 9781459756984 (PDF) | ISBN 9781459756991 (EPUB)
Subjects: LCSH: Dixon, Lance B.—Family. | LCSH: Canada. Canadian Army. Construction Battalion, 2—History. | LCSH: World War, 1914-1918—Regimental histories—Canada. | LCSH: Black people—Canada—History—20th century. | LCSH: World War, 1914-1918—Canada. | CSH: World War, 1914-1918—Participation, Black Canadian. | CSH: Black Canadians—Biography.
Classification: LCC D547.C2 D59 2026 | DDC 940.4/1271—dc23

We acknowledge the support of the Canada Council for the Arts and the Ontario Arts Council for our publishing program. We also acknowledge the financial support of the Government of Ontario, through the Ontario Book Publishing Tax Credit and Ontario Creates, and the Government of Canada.

Printed and bound in Canada.

Dundurn Press
1382 Queen Street East
Toronto, Ontario, Canada M4L 1C9
dundurn.com, @dundurnpress

To my father, and all other storytellers, who make us wiser because their tales reveal the truth of where we came from, who we are now, and what we are capable of becoming.

CONTENTS

The Dixon Family*

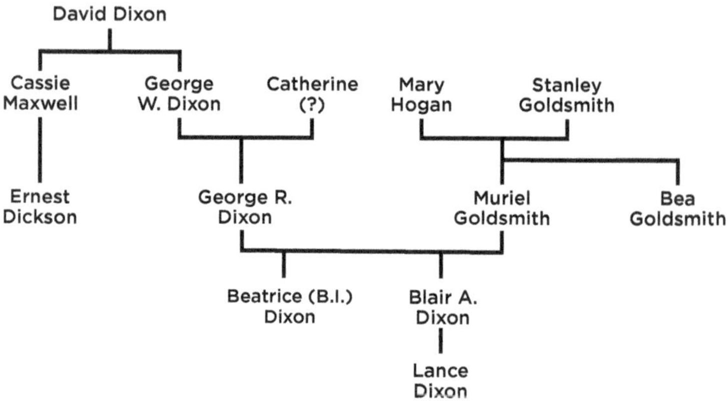

* This family tree includes only those members of the Dixon family featured in the book.

PREFACE

When I first sat down with my father to collectively capture a detailed account of how my grandfather George Dixon came to be one of six hundred men who fought in the only segregated Black Canadian battalion in the First World War, I really wanted his story to be an inspiring tale of courageous achievements against all the odds. A real underdog hero is what I imagined my grandfather to be, a character who could be a poster child for his generation. But the person who emerged from the pieces I collected turned out not to be a storybook hero at all. What I discovered, though, was a story of equal importance to tell. Yes, across his lifetime there were some incredible things my grandfather accomplished, from being a soldier to trying to raise a family during a time of oppression, that were tremendously challenging for anyone to face. In the end, what he offered was a poignant portrayal of what we all face along our human journey: the startling and sometimes painful contradictions of hope and heartache, power and prejudice, love and loneliness, fear and freedom.

To say he's not a war hero is not to diminish the role he played in one of the most remarkable tales in Canadian history. A whole class of men, denied their right to serve in the military for no other reason than the colour of their skin, defied the prejudice of a society that refused to see the irony of forcing men to fight for the right to protect the freedom of others in a distant land. So strong was the call to prove their worth as equals in society that recruits came from across Canada, and even from the United States, to form a battalion large enough to be mobilized for war. Among them was my grandfather, who, as I learned, signed up for no great noble purpose save friendship. He sacrificed a tremendous amount for his friends, and afterward he lived out his remaining days trying to reconcile the cost of fighting for a freedom that these Black soldiers never fully achieved back home. It was another generation who found the collective strength to finally reclaim the legacy of their courage. It is my hope, through this portrayal of my grandfather George Dixon, a man who died deeply wounded by the struggles of life, that we can appreciate how deeply racism affects those who have had to endure it.

My grandfather died when I was ten years old, and I shared few words with him. This account of my grandfather's life and role in the historic No. 2 Construction Battalion is told largely through the memory of my father, Blair Dixon, who was the last surviving of thirteen siblings, and one of the last direct descendants of the soldiers who fought in the Black Battalion in the First World War. Sadly, he passed away a week before completing this manuscript. For the various pieces of information my father could not recollect, or had no knowledge of, I am indebted to the dedicated few who have spent years collecting evidence of these men, as well as to various archival records that I spent long hours poring over. There were some key parts to the story that I simply could not put together without having to imagine how the events unfolded. To the reader, I ask that you simply imagine these moments with me as I attempt to bring the characters to life, as these stories become important strands that help weave the disparate pieces of my grandfather's life into a complete narrative. I have also changed some people's names so as not to misrepresent them in my telling of the tale. At the same time, there are other people whose names are kept as they really are, due to their significance outside of my grandfather's life.

In the end, the purpose of this book is not to present a detailed and comprehensive history of the No. 2 Construction Battalion. If the reader is interested in that kind of account, I highly recommend the late Senator Calvin Ruck's book, *The Black Battalion 1916–1920: Canada's Best Kept Military Secret.* Instead, I wanted to bring a very personal light to the historic events my grandfather was a part of. By sharing the many intimate conversations I had with my father, and my own critical reflections on the impact my grandfather's life had on the generations after him, I wanted to add a voice to our nation's narrative often not heard. Hopefully, through this tale of George Dixon, my grandfather, we can appreciate that every strand in the tapestry of our nation's history reflects a unique story born from the aspirations and struggles, heartaches and hopes of individuals whose names we may not know, but whose lives have enriched our nation nonetheless.

INTRODUCTION

Reckoning with Race

Not everything that is faced can be changed,
but nothing can be changed until it is faced.
—JAMES BALDWIN, "As Much Truth as One Can Bear"

Well, at least there is one moment I can look forward to in this purgatory of a daily commute. As the Deerfoot Trail expressway winds through the heart of Calgary, it takes a wide curve west onto the Calf Robe Bridge, which crosses the swift currents of the Bow River. In that instant, the majestic range of the Rocky Mountains appears straight ahead on the horizon, their snow-capped peaks piercing the sun setting behind them. Each day, I gratefully breathe in this brief display of creation's glory, just as the road quickly twists south again through the urban sprawl of the city.

On this particular day, though, my ritual moment of gratitude is interrupted by the phone ringing through the car speaker.

I press the talk button. "Hello, it's Lance here."

"Son," the voice rings through the speaker, "it's your father. I wanted you to know, the apology — it's happening."

My father's words immediately pull my attention away from the horizon, and I find myself staring back into a long and dark history of this nation. My father is referring to an apology that has finally been promised by the federal government for the discrimination that my grandfather George Dixon, along with six hundred other men, endured as soldiers of the only segregated Black battalion of the First World War. As descendants of Black folk in this country, it is not lost on us that it will be the first formal apology for *any* discrimination experienced by our people at the hands of the federal government. Recently, the government has initiated a litany of apologies for its unjust treatment of certain groups. The first was in 1988, when the Mulroney government apologized for the internment of Japanese Canadians during the Second World War. Since then, there have been official apologies to Indigenous people for the residential schools, to the Inuit for their forced relocation and the killing of their sled dogs, to the LGBTQ community for state-sanctioned discrimination in the workplace, to Chinese descendants for imposing an immigrant "head tax," and so on. It seems, at last, it is our turn.

"Is this for real?" I ask. "How do you know?"

"I got a call from Carol who helps run the Black history museum of Saskatchewan. She just got off the phone with a senior officer in the military. The date is already set, July 9th of next summer. It will mark the time they formed the battalion …"

My dad's voice falls quiet.

"Now that it's finally happening, how do you feel?" I ask him.

Another moment of silence passes before he slowly replies, "Truth be told, I never believed it would happen in my lifetime. And now that it has come … it just doesn't seem right that I would be the one to hear it. And really, of all his sons, I'm sure I would have been the last one my father would have chosen to stand before the prime minister of Canada on his behalf — but that's another story."

George Dixon was most commonly referred to as "Papa" among his descendants, my father included. It reflects the generational distance even some of his own thirteen children felt in the presence of this elusive father figure. From an early age, I knew about Papa and his role in the battalion because a portrait of him as a member of its marching band sat on the edge of the hutch in our living room. Strangely enough, as prominent as that image was in the memory of my childhood, I knew very little about what happened to him during the war. No doubt it was very difficult for my father, or any in his generation, to tell the story without reliving the painful racism they endured, and the shame they were taught to feel about being Black bodies in "a white man's world," as they were so often told. It has taken a whole generation to find the collective strength to bring to light the painful irony of their struggle, that these men had to fight their own country for the right to fight for the freedom of others in a distant land. In effect, white society refused to see the *souls* of these human beings who, possessing hope and heartache, bravery and brokenness, simply desired to be treated as men like any other.

In fairness, if they had taught about the legacy of the Black Battalion in Canadian schools, I wasn't around to hear it. Growing up as a biracial boy in Detroit during the '70s, in the wake of race riots that literally burned through that city, there was no need for a history lesson to learn about the reality of racism. We were all too aware of the violence that still plagued a divided America across colour lines. And that reality quickly shaped my identity. Many states were still holding on to laws that defined people according to their racial heritage, even though the federal government had signed the Civil Rights Act six years prior to my birth. It didn't matter that I was a light-skinned kid born of a white mother. Because my father was Black, the state defined me as Black. Those around me didn't question it, for by then racial identity had become more than simply the colour of one's skin. Over the generations, race became as much about the collective culture and consciousness of existing as *other than* white.

And the idea of "whiteness" in America was exclusive. So exclusive, in fact, that in the early days of constructing racial classes in America, even Europeans who were not of Anglo-Saxon descent were considered "non-whites." For instance, as the Irish showed up on the shores of America in the wake of the famine that impoverished their land (which many historians argue was the result of relentless colonial exploitation of their agriculture by the English), they were deemed by the British upper class as "European negroes." Initially, they were pushed into the same ghettoes as the Black and the Jewish people in the lower streets of New England cities.

In a short time, however, a vast number of Europeans gave up their distinct languages and cultures to assimilate into the upper class of English-speaking white America. In my current work as a racial equity educator, we try to foster classrooms as places where students can reclaim their identities by learning about diverse histories, in order to reimagine a future in which they truly belong. Ironically, it is often white teachers and students who struggle the most with the exercise, for so many of their ancestors deliberately erased their own sense of history to be "normalized" in a racially segregated society.

And make no mistake, those laws of segregation were powerful in shaping society. They predetermined where people grew up, the kind of schools they attended, and the places where people worked and shopped. And nowhere was the segregated landscape of America more evident than at eleven o'clock on Sunday morning. The phenomenon of "Black" churches, of "Chinese" and "Spanish" congregations, betrays the painful reality that even our religious denominations were complicit in shaping a racially segregated society. Very few white Americans can imagine church being any different from what it looks like through their own cultural lens. For instance, folk attending white suburban churches may be puzzled to hear that inside the front doors of our church in urban Detroit, there hung a large picture of a Black man with an Afro hair style. Every one of us kids knew that was Jesus greeting us when we walked through the door. If anyone questioned that, they'd be met with an indignant glare — "How *else* would Jesus look?"

My father would tell you that life had meaning for him in Detroit. This was the early '70s, and he had become the producer of two popular locally syndicated television shows and was surrounded by creative and energetic people. He was also the pastor of a congregation that was consciously engaged in the social struggle of the day. Grace Episcopal Church was situated right across the street from a "blind pig," the infamous after-hours club in this predominantly Black neighbourhood that was raided by police late one night in July 1967. Dozens were arrested, hundreds more poured onto the street in protest, and before anyone knew what happened, the building was ablaze. It was the spark that set the city on fire, ignited by deep frustration over decades of systemic racism, police brutality, and lack of opportunity, leading to five days of intense civil unrest. The violence left forty-three people dead, thousands arrested, and large parts of the city destroyed, marking one of the most destructive uprisings in U.S. history.

Rev. Blair Dixon with his sons, Beau (left) and Lance (right).

Through his countless hours of working in the community, Dad was deeply aware of the unresolved racial conflict that still gripped Detroit. Over time, my parents watched the "white flight" to the suburbs, which sadly included some of their own acquaintances. Though the exodus of white families from urban neighbourhoods had already quietly begun, the 1967 riots accelerated their departure from the city, as many associated the unrest with declining safety and property values. Discriminatory real estate practices like "blockbusting" stoked panic, convincing white homeowners to sell quickly before other races took over their neighbourhoods. At the same time, the loss of manufacturing jobs and the growth of suburban housing developments made moving more appealing. Together, these factors led to a mass migration of white residents to surrounding suburbs, deepening racial segregation and economic decline in Detroit. They took their economic wealth that could have been a valuable asset to rebuilding communities. Instead, public institutions, like the education system, were decimated. My parents, for example, couldn't afford private schools, which left them no choice but to deal with the upheaval happening in our local schools.

As the future became less certain, my parents made the hard decision to move back to Canada. My mom was raised in a quiet working-class neighbourhood on the east coast of Canada, and I suspect she thought it would be a better place to raise kids. In many ways she was right, but it turns out

In the Detroit Riots of 1967, violence resulted in forty-three deaths and the destruction of over two thousand buildings. Over 7,200 arrests were made during the unrest.

racism doesn't just stop at the border, and there were still hard lessons to be learned on how to face it. I was around nine years old when my father found work as a summer camp director for kids outside of London, Ontario. At first, I was shocked by how *confused* people in London seemed to be about race. This city existed in the heart of what was called Upper Canada during colonial times, whose society was meticulously built on the values of white Anglo-Saxon Protestantism, euphemistically referred to as WASP culture.

I was suddenly faced with navigating a society dominated by white people, many of whom seemed to carry a latent prejudice against anything that did not resemble old colonial England. Strangers seemed concerned about knowing "*What* are you?" and "Where are your parents *from*?" This left me feeling self-conscious of the fact that I looked a little different from their children. It was also common for kids to point out that I talked different — apparently, I slurred my *l*'s and twanged my *a*'s. My parents seemed oblivious to these things (little did I know the challenges they were facing as a mixed-race couple), and I didn't know how to talk about it with them. And school, well, that was the last place I thought to discuss my struggles about race and identity.

In fact, as a boy, timid and unsure of myself, "passing white" became my survival tool when I was at school. I will never forget the day I witnessed a group of kids surrounding a girl by the lockers during recess. She was a kid of an immigrant African family, and the only visible Black girl in our elementary school. The other kids had begun to ridicule her, calling her "darkie" and callously joking that she would taste like chocolate if she didn't look like — well, you get the idea. I retreated in silence. When I got home, I went to the bathroom and locked the door. I proceeded to take a bar of Ivory soap from the bathtub and rub it furiously into my skin. I was determined to remove any last vestiges of dark pigment I had.

Alas, after the third day of doing this, rashes started to appear all over my skin. They got so itchy I finally relented and took a bath. I recall sitting there for a long time, staring at the ceiling and soaking in my self-pity. Looking back, I'm filled with sadness that I had so quickly learned to look with shame on my Blackness. Why was I so desperate to fit into a society created to exclude people? Perhaps it was enough to have experienced, even marginally, the uncomfortableness of being labelled "other" and "different."

Not long after my failed attempt at whitening my skin with Ivory soap, our family moved to another neighbourhood. A few days after we unpacked our boxes, I took my bike out for a ride. I was about a block down the street when a boy approached me on his bike.

"Hey," he shouted as he coasted to a stop. "You new on the block? What's your name?"

To this day, I feel the intense anxiety that clenched my throat as I looked into the eyes of this kid staring back at me. To him, the question was quite simple. In me, however, his words touched a deep nerve. It evoked the far more complicated question that was causing something of a crisis in my young mind. My hands held more tightly onto the handlebars as I blankly stared back at him. *What are you?* That was the real question I heard him ask me.

In complete desperation I blurted out, "Mike — my name is Mike."

Of course, the inevitable happened. Later that Saturday morning, I was sitting at the kitchen table mindlessly eating my cereal when someone knocked on our front door. I heard my mom get up from her chair in the living room and open it. In the instant I heard the boy's voice, my spoon froze halfway to my mouth. After the boy asked my mom if Mike could come out and play, I heard my mother in a puzzled tone explain that no one by the name of Mike lived here. As the door closed, I waited with dread for my mother to appear in the kitchen. She never came.

The next day the kid caught up with me at the end of the street. "So, what's up? Do you live in that house or not?"

I shrugged, then nodded.

With the same puzzled look with which I'm sure my mom had looked at him, he continued, "But the lady said you didn't live there ..." Again the boy stared at me.

Finally, I muttered, "Oh, you mean my mom? Well, my name *is* Lance. But I prefer Mike — you know, like a nickname ..."

It didn't change the bewildered look on the boy's face. Eventually, as if the summer day was too good to waste on nonsensical conversation, he shrugged his shoulders and jumped back on his bike. As I began pedalling off behind him, an overwhelming feeling of stupidity came over me. Really, *Mike*? What was I thinking? Truth is, how could I expect him to understand that I just wanted to be normal? After all, no one in the world except me was named *Lance* — it only reminded me of being different. I mean, who names their child *Lance*, anyway? Parents who are *different* — that's who. At least with a name like Mike, I had hoped there'd be one less thing that was different about me. *Different* meant being surrounded in the back of a coat room, or being ridiculed and rejected. No thanks; I was happy to pretend to be someone else.

When I was with my father in strange places though, I couldn't avoid it. I will never forget one time on the Munsee-Delaware First Nation reserve, about a forty-minute drive west of the city. My father, being the only man of colour in his religious denomination, was often sent there to provide religious services to the "Indians," as his bishop called them. One day, he decided to take me along. I recall driving up the long country road until at last we reached the high wooden gate entrance into the reserve. Among the sparse scattering of buildings there was a church that also functioned as a community centre. After the service, I wandered down the hallway to where it opened up into a gym and found a bunch of boys of various ages playing a game of pick-up floor hockey. I stood in the doorway for a few minutes watching them. I could see some of them looking over at me. Feeling a little self-conscious just standing there by myself, I picked up a stick and started idly slapping a ball against the side of the wall. Eventually, a couple of the older boys walked toward me.

"What are you doing here?" one curiously asked.

Not sure how to respond, I shrugged and said, "I dunno, I came with my dad."

"Who's your dad?" he pressed further.

Assuming the kid hadn't sat through the church service, I wasn't sure how to explain it to him. As it turned out, I didn't need to come up with an answer, because in that moment my dad walked into the gym.

"Oh, there you are, son," he called out. "I'm almost done, meet me at the car in five minutes, will you?" My dad glanced over at the boys standing next to me, gave a wave, and disappeared.

The boy turned to me. "Is *that* your dad?"

"Yeah," I faintly replied. "That's my dad."

And then his look changed in a way that I had seen so often in others. "Oh, so you a *n****r*, then?"

And of course, I responded as I usually did in the many uncomfortable moments of being *othered* — I laughed it off. It felt so weak, so disingenuous, to smile and pretend it didn't matter to me that people needed to point out I was *not* like them. Especially here, I thought, in a community literally shaped by centuries of racial prejudice and exploitation, people could still not imagine our relationships apart from the social *otherness*. On the ride home to the city, I sat in the back seat with a dejected feeling. It would be nice to show up *somewhere* in the world and not have to explain myself, to simply exist in spaces without having to justify why I am there. The next day I woke up and went to school. As I walked into the crowded hallways of students and headed to my first class, I tried to put what happened the day before into the back of my mind. After all, looking around my classroom, who in this place would even relate to what I experienced? I doubted any of them, including the teacher, had been to the Munsee-Delaware reserve, if they even knew it existed. *Just forget about it*, I said to myself, *and move on*. That was the best advice I could give myself at the time.

School, however, kept reminding me that race was an unavoidable aspect of our identity in this society. For instance, years later I was sitting in a grade 12 English class among some thirty other students. The teacher, an older white man with grey hair greased back, had a habit of picking random students to read characters as they popped up in our novel studies. I'll never forget the moment, while reading *The Adventures of Huckleberry Finn*, when Huck and Tom come across a "slave" named Jim. The teacher turned to me and said, "Lance I understand your father is Black, read the part of Jim." Now, I had paid enough attention to know that the setting of the book was an old southern town in Missouri. What could a kid from an urban city in the industrial north know about life there? But this teacher was now glaring over at me, and I looked around to see thirty kids shooting curious glances in my direction.

So, I tried to speak the lines like a southerner from the 1800s. Not two sentences into the paragraph the teacher cut me off, "Well — seems I was mistaken, you have no idea how a Black person talks," and abruptly pointed to another student for him to continue. For the rest of the class, I mostly just looked down at my desk, first working through my embarrassment, then confusion as to how this teacher thought a Black person ought to talk, and then anger that a white man with greased-back hair even got to decide. Needless to say, I didn't put much effort into his course after that.

As you can imagine, I had no thought of becoming a teacher when I was in school. But life has a way of coming full circle, and here I now am, determined to foster classrooms in which every student can explore their authentic sense of identity in a positive light. I was recently invited to speak during a high school student leadership conference here in Calgary on the topic of "creating welcoming schools." All the schools represented were publicly funded Catholic schools from across the city, so at one point I opened the Bible, and read these words: "In Christ, there is neither Jew nor Greek, slave nor free, male nor female — for we are all one in Christ Jesus." These words, I reminded the participants, were written just a few years after Jesus's death by one of his followers, Paul, in his letter to a fledgling church in Galatia in the heart of the Roman Empire. As this struggling church was still figuring out how to follow Jesus's message of love, Paul wrote these words as a vision for what the community *could* become — for even back then people were divided along these very lines. The truth is, I pointed out, social division is nothing new to the human race, and for the past two thousand years we have witnessed the tragedy of the failure to free ourselves from our inherent prejudice against those who are different. Tireless though it may be, we all must do our part to change the way we see one another.

I pulled into the driveway and stopped the car.

"Dad," I said, "it's time we tell Papa's story."

1

Life at the End of Campbell Road

> At negro point, some forgot sleep,
> sang "oh freedom over me"
> heard mournful trains cry like blizzards
> along blue bedford basin . . .
> none do now.
>
> —GEORGE ELLIOTT CLARKE,
> "Campbell Road Church"

It's an early autumn evening in Calgary, the year 2021. After a long day I finally find a moment to call Dad to continue our conversation from the day before. My father, Blair Allison Dixon, had moved to Regina almost thirty years ago, leaving me and my two siblings with our mother two provinces away. To this day, I'm not sure what compelled him to seek a new life in the middle of the prairies thousands of miles from anyone he knew. I suppose I could have asked him, but there never seemed much point in figuring it out. My siblings and I eventually came to accept that this small prairie city is where Dad felt most content to continue his life. He was taken on as a pastor of a church in an older part of downtown and, to his credit, tirelessly served that parish until at last the bishop forced him to retire on his seventy-second birthday. That, too, was many years ago. Six months ago, he turned eighty-six.

Since his retirement, time has not been kind to my father. He was once an agile and athletic man — a basketball star at Acadia University in the late '50s, an athlete on the national track team, and a boxer competing for the Canadian Air Force during his four years of service. Now, he can barely move, so debilitated is he by severe arthritis throughout his joints. You ask him about his condition and he will insist that, as a result of his rigorous physiotherapy routine, he's getting the better of it. My siblings and I, however, watch the steady decline, and endure the tension caused by his stoic disposition.

For instance, his refusal to use his walker to get from one room to the next puts others constantly on edge with the prospect of him falling — which has occurred more times that anyone cares to admit. We've been out in public, and even complete strangers have instinctively jumped toward my father with genuine anxiety on their faces as he stumbles and sways across the sidewalk. And, without fail, they look at us walking next to him with a confused and incredulous stare, wondering why we seem content leaving this old man to fend for himself. Of course, they don't know that we already tried to intervene a few times, but to no avail. There is a part of me that understands my father's stubborn attempt at overcompensating for weakness or vulnerability. It's ingrained in the male psyche, especially among those of my father's generation. Even still, growing up it was hard for any of us to live under his stoic rules of life.

At the same time, as a boy I was also proud to have a father who others looked up to. Being part of a historic Black congregation, he was afforded a certain reverence as a pastor, which I sensed. And he earned his congregation's respect all the more for his measured approach to the complex issues they had to face during the early '70s. In the aftermath of the race riots in Detroit, there were conflicting views about how to rebuild the neighbourhoods, and the congregation of Grace Episcopal was a microcosm of those divided opinions. A number of people wanted the church to become a beacon of "integration" as a means of promoting more investment in the community on the part of white businesses. On the other hand, a growing number of younger members were becoming disillusioned with the social agenda of racial integration, and they started taking a more militant approach to protecting the interests of Black communities.

Initially, the church building was opened to youth to start a Black Power movement, and then the church leaders agreed to a mural, the *Wall of Pride*, being painted on the wall of the church overlooking the newly renamed Rosa Parks Boulevard. It was, in hindsight, a project not entirely thought out. The artists, an eclectic group of individuals from the wider community, ended up portraying an equally eclectic and vast array of Black activists throughout history, some of whom were not without controversy: Dr. King was painted right alongside Albert Cleage, the founder of a militant Black Power movement, while Moses, the Hebrew prophet from the Old Testament, was depicted just opposite Elijah Muhammad, the founder of the Nation of Islam for Black nationalists in local Detroit! Needless to say, such a mural displayed prominently on a church building along a major boulevard running through this part of the city became a lightning rod for community conflict.

After months of growing tension around this mural, my father got a call one early morning from the church caretaker. In the middle of the night, someone had covered the whole mural with white paint. Suddenly, my father was faced with a full-on crisis, thrown into the unenviable position of mediating a fractious town hall meeting with furious allegations being cast on both sides. My father made every effort to reconcile the fighting groups and help chart a path forward. However, to this day the mystery of who was responsible

Painted on an exterior wall of Grace Episcopal Church, the *Wall of Pride* mural became an iconic image of Black pride in the city of Detroit.

for the erasure of the infamous mural remains. Interestingly enough, two art historians from the University of Michigan recently tracked down my father to learn more of the fateful circumstances surrounding this mural, which has now become an iconic image of the history of the city.

In the midst of all this, come Sunday morning, my father was expected to bring the whole congregation together. Especially during those tumultuous times, there was no hour more important than eleven o'clock on Sunday morning. Too much was at stake in the lives of those sitting in the pews for a pastor to just "punch the clock." Many people mistake the flamboyance of Black pastors as being for entertainment value. Sure, there's an element of theatrics that is brought to the moment, but in its most authentic form it is the spirit-filled prophetic tradition of proclaiming a transcendent word of hope to a people who have lived in oppression for too long.

Now, my father never strayed too far from his intellectual disposition, but he leaned into the cadence and crescendos of a well-delivered sermon just the same. On virtually every Sunday of my childhood I sat in a pew just a few feet in front of him, sandwiched between my mother and older sister (my brother and I were kept apart for good reason). Despite being preoccupied with having to sit uncomfortably with a tie wrapped around my neck when I could be watching cartoons, I was constantly aware of my father's presence. As I look back, it was the congregation's spontaneous response behind me that was most impressive. I would watch them listen to my father, and as they clapped and clattered I would turn and watch my father respond in sync with a timely word that only spurred them on. From my pew below him, I marvelled at my father's ability to orchestrate this spiritual symphony. Clearly, he had the ability to stir people's souls and, even as a young boy, it gave me a sense of pride.

These are the memories I have in my mind when I hear my father speak now. Over the many years, his role as a father and pastor created a complex, and sometimes contradictory, figure in our family. As I prepare to call him, though, I am also aware that in the years since he left, many miles apart from one another, I have come to simply accept my father for who he is, and even to love him.

I grab a glass of water and settle into my small office. I pull out a pad of paper from the drawer and dial my dad's number.

"Hello, son, is that you?" I hear him fumbling with his headset.

"Yeah, Dad, I'm here," I respond, and then patiently wait.

Recently, my dad's arthritis has gotten so bad that he can no longer hold on to the phone. It has become something of a ritual to listen to the crackling and rustling of the headset against his chin while he struggles to get it in place.

"There," he says at last. "I'm all ready."

"No problem, how's your day been?"

"Oh," he replies flatly, "today was a good day."

"Good to hear." Expecting to get little else on that topic, I quickly move on. "So, let's start at the beginning, Dad. You've mentioned before that your own father never talked about his parents. Why is that? Is there anything you know about them?"

"Well," my father begins, "what little I did hear was from Aunt Bea, our mama's younger sister. My word, that woman could talk, and I know it drove Mama crazy at times! When I was young, Aunt Bea would always come to visit Mama, and they would talk non-stop — and by that

I mean Aunt Bea would talk while Mama listened. They would start at the table, then move to the front stoop, then to the clothesline behind the house, and then down the street as Aunt Bea followed Mama to the market. And it'd be quiet for a while, until sure enough we could hear from the end of the street the chatter of Aunt Bea as she followed Mama back to the house!"

As off-topic as it was, listening to my dad recall the larger-than-life character of my great-aunt Bea made me curious.

"On the topic of Aunt Bea," I chime in, "how did she learn so much about the family while the rest knew so little?"

"Well," my dad says matter-of-factly, "she made it her business to know these things, and she had ample opportunity to hear the gossip from up and down the east coast. Completely opposite to Mama, who had thirteen children, Aunt Bea had none. She spent her free time frequenting many of our Black communities, including Africville in Nova Scotia, which at the time was a real hotbed of musical talent. You may recall, Aunt Bea fancied herself as an entertainer, and never missed a chance to associate herself with the in-crowd wherever she went. At any rate, she never failed to return with some new gossip she was excited to share with Mama."

"But in all her talking," my dad continues, "she had very little to say about Papa's parents. She seemed certain they had arrived by ship at some point from the eastern coast of the United States, when your papa was still an infant. No doubt

Aunt Bea was deeply curious as to why they fled the States, or where they disappeared to after leaving Papa in Africville when he was just a boy. However, she avoided bringing up the topic of Papa's parents in his presence — it was clear being abandoned was something he never got over. Save Jean, my third-eldest sister, who tried to take after Aunt Bea in more ways than one, the rest of us just left it alone. We figured the mystery of his parents would always remain just that ..."

My dad goes silent on the other end of the phone, then whispers, "That is, until last week."

It takes me a second to catch on. "Wait, what happened last week?"

"Well," my father explains, "your cousin Eunice called me the other day, very excited. The husband of one of her clients at the hair salon is a retired military man, and he's now doing genealogical research for families of deceased soldiers. So, Eunice asked him to see what he could find about your papa. As he was looking through George's old military personnel files, he came across one document which asked about the identity of the soldier's parents. Apparently, George simply stated that he had a father, also named George, living somewhere in Rhode Island, and that his mother wasn't alive."

I am now leaning halfway out of my chair, trying to process this new development in the story.

"That's crazy," I respond. "Your father knew about his parents all along ... but didn't tell anyone?"

My father chuckles softly. "Yes, it seems that was the case. Looking back, the whole time he preferred to let people wonder and guess who his real parents were, rather than tell them the truth. I suppose it brings to light just how bitter my father was for being abandoned by them."

I am suddenly overcome with a sense of sadness for my grandfather. It's heartbreaking to think that he preferred to live as if those who brought him into this world never existed. At the same time, I'm also struck by how important this man's research was for our family. I quickly scribble on my note pad, "Dig into archives" and then return to the phone call.

"So," I continue, "Papa began life as an orphan in Africville … do you know much about his time there?"

"That his life there was not a happy one," my dad answers bluntly.

"Why do you say that?" I ask.

"First of all," my father remarks, "your papa ran away from there pretty much any chance he got. One time, and this is a story your great-aunt Bea did tell quite often, Papa disappeared from Africville when he was six years old. Eventually, they found him in Boston."

"Boston?" I exclaim. "But that's across the ocean. How did a six-year-old manage that?"

I ponder the fact that our grandfather experienced more in his childhood than what many have in a lifetime. I start to imagine how he accomplished such a remarkable feat, one achieved only by great courage — or sheer desperation. Either way, my curiosity leads me to more questions.

"So," I ask, "who found him in Boston?"

There is a brief silence over the phone before Dad replies, "Let me see, yes, a woman by the name of Angeline Dixon."

"Ah," I surmise, "so someone from the house where George grew up in Africville?"

"Not really," my father slowly responds, as if trying to sort out pieces of a puzzle in his head. "It's a little complicated, but at this point in time there were two families living in Africville who went by the last name of Dixon — and they happened to live right next door to each other. As far as anyone knew, there was no relationship between the two families. Now, Angeline was part of the *other* Dixon household … although she was technically not a Dixon. Angeline was a *Jarvis* actually, a descendant of one of the earliest families to settle the Black Loyalist community of Weymouth Falls, on the west side of Nova Scotia. She married Joseph, the son of Allen and Sarah Dixon, who lived next door to the Dixons where George was living."

"You're right," I mutter, "this is a little confusing."

Dad ignores my critique of his storytelling and presses on. "Now the head of the Dixon household where George lived was Josiah. He had a wife named Ethel, and three children, all grown by the time George appeared on the scene.

Again, how George came to live with these Dixons is a bit of a mystery. And I really didn't know much more about this family, for Papa never spoke a word about them. But again, Africville was a small enough settlement to find out these things, if you really made it your business to know, like Aunt Bea did. I actually spent some time in Africville myself after I had left home, but many of the families during my father's time had long since left."

My dad didn't need to explain the circumstances surrounding the painful demise of Africville. From its beginning, Halifax had always neglected the care of the Black settlement, but by the late '50s, city officials were actively forcing the longtime residents off their properties, as they coveted this once-forsaken land for industrial development projects. At first, the city refused to provide the most basic services to the community, but by the early '60s, officials resorted to physically bulldozing homes, sending families out on to the streets. By 1967, Africville had been demolished. In the midst of such trauma, as people dispersed to live in other communities, there was little time to gather the memories of how Africville used to be, although thanks to some, the old Seaview Church was resurrected and now serves as a living museum of this settlement. And outside of its doors, one resident has returned to live on the land. His name is Eddie Carvery, a descendant of one of the families who originally founded the settlement. Years after his house was demolished,

Children playing in Africville, where there was little access to fresh water.

Carvery defiantly parked a trailer on his old property and, to this day, refuses to leave, despite multiple eviction notices. His singular presence remains an enduring witness to our independent way of life on this small piece of land when all other evidence was razed to the ground.

I wanted to get back to these Dixon families, and the story of my grandfather running away to Boston, but in that moment another call came through. Before hanging up, I assured Dad that I would be in touch again very soon. Later that evening I began searching online to learn more of the background behind these events in Papa's life. Africville was originally known as the Campbell Road settlement, for it sat at the end of this same road that wound a few miles north from Halifax to the edge of the Bedford Basin. It's not clear where the name "Africville" came from, but it stuck with the residents, and since the 1900s that's what everyone called it. It was a tiny collection of homes that were propped up on the steep slopes overlooking the ocean, the community divided by the rail tracks that ran through it from Halifax Harbour and up the coast. Over the generations, the families dug deep roots along those rocky shores and managed to build a school, a general store, and, most impressively, the Seaview Baptist Church, which quickly became the heart and soul of the community.

Traditional berry picking in a field above Africville.

My dad had guessed that Papa was born in 1895 and was somehow brought to this settlement shortly afterward. I begin searching all the digital archives I can find for the names "Dixon" or "George" in the years before and after, and even throw in his middle name, "Richard," for good measure. After looking for hours without finding any reference to him being born there, I figure Great-Aunt Bea was correct, that my grandfather had indeed been brought across the ocean as an infant. But I want to make sure, so I follow the same pattern of searching for George Dixon, this time in the census records, one year forward and one year back. Here, at last, I find his name! In the 1901 census, under the household of a "Josiah and Ethel Dixson," and alongside three adult-aged children, there was a six-year-old boy listed by the name of George.

Interestingly, George is listed as a *son* of Josiah and Ethel. So why had his name not come up before when I searched for this family? I decide to look ahead to see how often his name appeared with this family, but there is no record of him in the following census of 1906. In fact, I can't find a record of George anywhere. He appears again in the 1911 census under this same household in Africville. This time, however, George is listed as the *grandson* of Josiah and Ethel. Needless to say, it raises a lot of suspicions about his real relationship to this family. If my grandfather had indeed been born to this couple, or to any of their adult children, they had provided no birth certificate or baptism record, nor included him in the previous census of 1896, when he would have been born. I consider that maybe my grandfather's age was marked incorrectly, and that he simply could have been born to this family at a different time and place. But this Dixon family showed up in census records for the previous thirty years, living at the same address in Africville.

At the same time, several other children are randomly listed in this house on different census records through the years — and by the next census there is no trace of them. George, it seems, was not the only one for whom they tried to provide a home. And, like George, none of them stayed very long. I suspect the failure to provide a stable home for orphaned children was the result of a troubling shadow hidden in the story of this family. It would at least explain why my grandfather was so desperate to leave. Of course, it still leaves his real parents as a mystery with no clear answers. I am starting to wonder if there are aspects of my grandfather's story I will never know. I sit with that thought for a moment, then close my computer. Something tells me that the most important questions are still to be asked.

2

The Feeling of Freedom

> For the caged bird
> sings of freedom.
> —MAYA ANGELOU, "Caged Bird"

Later that week I call my dad with what I have learned about the Dixon family who Papa lived with in Africville. He sits with this in silence for a bit.

"Well," he eventually whispers, "that all makes sense."

I'm eager to return to the story of my grandfather escaping across the ocean. "Dad, so tell me about Angeline Dixon, the woman who found six-year-old George in Boston."

"Well, I'll tell you what has been said of her, for it was before my time. She was a character almost out of a storybook, a real fairy godmother, at least as far as the tale of your grandfather goes. Angeline was immensely popular among the burgeoning Black middle-class women of Boston, for she had the gift of stitching the finest dress with just a few scraps of fabric. She could make any lady look like a princess at the cost of a pauper's coin. But it was not just her talents that endeared people to her. Angeline had a smile that left the room bright. She had an air of confidence that defied her otherwise lowly stature on the racially segregated streets of Boston."

"Now," my dad continues, "her husband Joseph spent his days working as a porter on the ferries between Boston and Yarmouth, Nova Scotia. They lived in a small apartment in Cambridge, across the river from Boston, but when Joseph was on leave from the ship they would often visit his parents in Africville. Angeline was known to love kids, and she took a special liking to your grandfather. I'm sure it had a lot to do with him being an orphan and all, but your great-aunt Bea did say your papa had a certain charm about him in his younger days.

"At any rate, your great-aunt Bea's story of George running away to Boston begins one early summer morning, when Angeline had come to visit her in-laws ..."

As my dad settles into the story, my eyes wander to the scenes being cast before me, like an old black and white movie being narrated by a voice full of colour. I picture what it would have been like for my grandfather, and all these characters, to play their part in this moment of time, hidden from history, yet now being brought to life in my father's telling of the tale. I imagine George, barely six years old, sitting on a hand-woven blanket in the rocky yard behind the Dixon house in Africville, diving into a bowl of freshly picked berries …

• • •

As Ethel sat next to George on the blanket, absent-mindedly watching him pick through the bowl of berries, she looked up to see Angeline, elegantly dressed, gliding through the bramble and shrubs toward them.

"Well," exclaimed Ethel, "What a pleasant surprise! I didn't hear you were planning to come by these parts."

"You're quite right," Angeline replied warmly, "it was unexpected to be sure. Joseph is on leave of his porter duties while the ferry is being refitted for parts here in Halifax."

"Oh," exclaimed Ethel, "but the ladies in Boston must be displeased, I'm sure of it."

Angeline laughed. "The ladies of Boston will never tire of new fashion. It won't take long for me to be busy again." And she added, "Besides, there's far more important things in life …"

Angeline lifted a basket toward Ethel. "Look what I brought you. Not me, mind you. It's extra stew beef and vegetables that Joseph's mother asked me to bring over."

"Y'all are far too kind, Angeline."

"Not at all." Angeline glanced over at the boy near Ethel's feet, then softly whispered, "Tell me … how you keeping?"

Ethel sighed deeply. "Well, let's see, my goodness I seem to have been quite busy of late …" She looked over at George. Turning back to Angeline, she feigned a smile. "I'm okay, really."

Angeline offered a brief smile in return, but she couldn't hide her concern. "Forgive me, your business is your own and I have no intention to pry … but I heard it's been hard for Josiah to get delivery routes."

"We're getting old, me and Josiah. I wonder if …" Her voice fell to a whisper as she turned her head away from George. "I wonder how long we can take care of him. Josiah just isn't himself these days."

Angeline smiled tenderly and laid a hand on Ethel's shoulder. "All I can say, Ethel, is that the boy is fortunate the good Lord brought him to your door. God only knows what his life may have become otherwise."

Angeline hugged her, then stooped down and rubbed George's nappy head of hair. "And you, little man, I'm going to come back and take you down to the swimming hole. I reckon some cool water would do my feet good."

George quickly shot his head up, a big, stained grin now covering his face. "I'll come with you, Auntie Angeline, I wouldn't want you to fall in the water!"

Angeline let out a laugh, "Well, what a gentleman — and a quick-witted one at that. All right, I'll come by, and you can take me down to the water." With a wink, Angeline turned and made her way back to the other Dixon house across the yard.

It was close to dinner when George wandered into the house after playing along the shore with Angeline. As George stepped through the door, he paused. The house was eerily quiet. He slowly made his way down the single hallway and stopped at the entrance of the kitchen. Ethel was standing in front of the counter with her back to George, staring out the small window that overlooked the yard. As George went to sit down at the table, Ethel spun around with an anxious look.

She breathed a sigh of relief when she saw it was him. "George, you scared me ..." As she returned her gaze out the window, she muttered, "I'm afraid he's been at Rollie's canteen for far too long now."

In silence, George watched Ethel move to the stove and set a fire. She then brought a jug of water over and poured it into a pot on the table. She went back to the counter, took the basket of food Angeline had brought over earlier that day, and sat next to George.

Without looking up, Ethel asked, "Would you like to cut these for me?"

George took the knife and started working on the vegetables as Ethel began cutting the beef into small chunks. They took turns placing food into the pot. When they were done, Ethel got up and placed the pot on the cook stove. As she slowly stirred the mixture of meat and vegetables, George quietly watched her. After a few minutes she put the ladle down and sat next to George. Neither appeared anxious to speak about anything.

The tranquility of the moment was disrupted by the front door being thrown open. Ethel instantly shot up as Josiah, her husband, stumbled into the kitchen. By now dusk had come over the settlement, and the fire within the stove cast a large shadow behind him. Ethel quickly moved over to the stove and glanced nervously behind her.

"Well, come on," she said, "have a seat. Dinner won't be too long."

Josiah was having trouble standing straight. He took a few wobbly steps toward her then stopped in the centre of the kitchen. George carefully watched as Josiah scanned the table. A deep furrow came over his brow as he set his eyes upon the rations. He lowered himself unsteadily into the chair across from the boy. George remained very still, not taking his eyes off Josiah. Ethel went over to grab plates off a shelf and place them on the table. She noticed Josiah staring at the extra food and turned back to the stove. She struggled to hide her nervousness.

"You must be wonderin' how it is I got all these rations," she said. "Well, Angeline brought them over —"

"Angeline, ha!" Josiah scowled. "She can't keep her nose where it belongs."

Ethel tensed. "Angeline cares about us is all, and you know how fond she is of George —"

"Is that so?" Josiah scoffed. "Then why don't she take the boy?"

Ethel kept her back to Josiah. "Now, you know we the only home the boy has —"

Josiah grimaced as he took a long hard stare at George, then lunged clumsily at the boy and pulled him from the chair. George recoiled from the stench of alcohol on Josiah's breath.

"This boy?" Josiah sneered as he turned again to Ethel. "Like the ones you brought home before? And what happened then Ethel, need I remind you? Let Angeline take care of him, if she such a saint. I'm done feedin' other people's kids."

Josiah started toward the back door, dragging the boy with him. George tried to pull himself away. Josiah turned, his eyes filled with rage, and slapped George across the face. The boy gasped, then flailed his arm and legs against Josiah. The older man threw a fist into the boy's side.

George bent over, clutching the edge of the table to keep himself from falling. Ethel leaped to the boy's defense, but she was too late. Josiah had flung George over the table and across the floor.

Ethel rushed to the corner of the kitchen where George lay motionless. Kneeling over him, she pleaded for the boy to get up. He groaned. As Ethel pulled George closer, he defiantly pushed himself away and staggered toward the door.

"George!" Ethel cried after him. "Please don't go. George — you come back here!"

Halfway through the door of the hallway, George turned back to look at Ethel, folded on the floor. Josiah stood in the centre of the kitchen, silent and cold as stone. George looked at Ethel one last time, then turned and disappeared into the night.

In the pale dusk he stumbled down the yard and onto the rail tracks. He ran east along the line, and soon the last wooden houses of the Campbell Road settlement faded into the darkness behind him. As the tracks veered south toward the city, he stepped off and pushed himself through the dense brush, stumbling down the ridge, until he came across a shed behind the slaughterhouse situated near the mouth of the basin. He flung the door open and threw himself across the damp straw covering the ground. Alone in the dark, the boy pounded his feet against the wall. A light was suddenly cast through the slats in the shed from the direction of the slaughterhouse. George quickly lay still, muffling his cries in the sleeve of his shirt. When the light finally vanished, the boy turned over and cried himself to sleep in the darkness.

The next morning, George was startled awake by the sound of a bell ringing in the distance. He squinted in the bright morning sunlight piercing through the thin walls. He drew a deep breath, then sat upright. Cautiously, George pushed the door open and stepped outside. Almost instantly, clean ocean air filled his lungs, and the warmth of the sun's rays soaked his ebony skin like a balm. In the blue sky above him, a gull swooped across the steep slopes and over the ocean water. He stood still as his eyes followed the flight of the bird. Then, the clang of the bell pulled him back to earth, and he headed in the direction from where it came.

He pushed himself through the brush and continued back along the tracks toward the settlement. Eventually, he stood in front of the Seaview Baptist Church, where the peal of the bell rang from its steeple. George slipped through the front doors and slid onto a bench in the far corner. On this particular morning, as voices lifted into the rafters and the organ rang out a rich melody, the sound of a trumpet rose above the chorus. George was compelled to perch himself just high enough on the bench to see a man swinging his brass instrument in rhythm with the swaying and clapping hands of the congregation.

Seaview Baptist Church in Africville, on the edge of the rail tracks overlooking the Bedford Basin.

At last, after a full morning of worship, the preacher exhaled a final crescendo of "glory" and "alleluia," and then beckoned the congregation outside for a picnic. George didn't hesitate. He joined the first stream of people toward the tables propped up in the yard and started scooping pastries and sandwiches into his shirt he had stretched out like a ragged canopy. By the time he got to the second cart, bodies were pressing in on him from every side. He spun and pirouetted around the crowd, gathering as much as he could before he would be out of reach of it entirely. George noticed a man placing the last slice of cheese on his serviette. As the man turned to chat with a fellow congregant,

George quickly snatched the cheese and dropped it into the fold of his shirt.

In that instant, he felt someone grab his elbow and twist him around. Caught in the sins of greed and gluttony, he looked up into the eyes of his prosecutor. It seems God's mercy was upon the boy, for Angeline stood before him.

"Well," Angeline said with a wry smile, "if it isn't my dear, sweet George."

George looked down into his shirt, and lifted the bundle toward Angeline as if to offer an atoning sacrifice. "Would you like one of my sandwiches?"

Angeline laughed. "No, something tells me you need it more than I do! But I'll tell you what," she continued, "I have a feeling there's a lot we need to catch up on. Let's find a spot to sit while you enjoy your spoils, shall we?"

George nodded. They left the churchyard and strolled down the road until they came to an opening overlooking the water. George sat down and spread his food upon his lap. Angeline sat next to him and watched George abandon himself to devouring every morsel he had gathered. When George seemed to have his fill, Angeline began peppering him with questions. Before long, she had pieced together much of what had transpired.

As George was swallowing the last of his food, they heard a voice behind them, "There you are, been looking all over for you!"

Joseph came bounding across the road and sat next to Angeline. He briefly studied little George sitting next to her. "And what company are you keeping, my lady?"

As he winked at George and Angeline smiled, Joseph continued, "Well, George. This is indeed a pleasant surprise. My wife wondered where you had disappeared to. And here you are!"

George looked down across the ocean. Seeing the boy staring off into the distance, Joseph leaned over and asked, "Have you ever thought of travelling the seas?"

George looked closer at the many vessels crossing through the narrows. Massive steamships churned the waters as billows of smoke trailed above. He marvelled at the sleek schooners skimming through the water. There were merchant ships and military cruisers, and smaller fishing trawlers, all traversing the open water like on a road with endless directions.

"No, sir," George wistfully replied.

Joseph joined the boy in gazing across the water. "Do you know why I love the sea, George?"

The boy shook his head. Joseph leaned closer and said softly, "When all the passengers retire from the decks, and the night is late, and the moon is the only light over the water, I stretch over the bow and listen to the rhythm of the waves." Joseph moved his hands as if they were swimming through the wind. "And in those moments, son, the land

and all its troubles seem so far away. I listen to the water below, parting before me like Moses standing before the Red Sea, and I feel … free."

They sat for a while on the slopes, looking over the ocean, as Joseph shared his joy of listening in on travellers recounting their many adventures overseas, of learning about exotic food, and of seeing strange artifacts come aboard the ships from foreign lands.

After Joseph and Angeline left him, George strode up and down the livestock trails that ran through the pastures on the high plateau to the west. He wandered the paths that connected fishing holes along the steep rocky shores. Sitting alone, he stared over the water again, watching the boats drift along the currents beneath him. Eventually, the shadows became long, and the wind cool, as the sun fell further away to the horizon. George stood up and started toward Angeline and Joseph's house.

He took the long way over the ridge, to avoid passing by Ethel and Josiah's house. Approaching from the back of the yard, George could hear Angeline and Joseph chattering in the front of their house. He sprinted around the corner. Joseph was standing on the edge of the steps, dressed in a black suit with large silver buttons fastened all the way up to a very high collar. Resting on his head was a stiff black cap with a shiny peak, and wide black pant legs fell straight down from his waist, covering his shoes. Angeline was crouched on the step below him, furiously trying to pin the bottom of the pant leg. Joseph teetered as he tried to peer over Angeline.

"How much longer, Angeline?" Joseph cried. "We gonna be late!"

"And it's my fault you waited so long to tell me you needed new pants?" Angeline retorted.

"Well," Joseph began to argue, "I thought I told you on the way here baby doll —"

But Angeline was having none of that. "Oh," she snapped, "Don't baby doll me, mister!"

George had been quietly listening to their bickering on the sidelines. Suddenly, he interjected, "Wait — where you going?"

In unison, Joseph and Angeline turned toward the direction of the boy's voice. George was staring back at them with an anxious look. Angeline put down her thread.

Joseph cleared his throat and gently replied, "Well — we're heading back to Boston, son. The boat's ready to go, you see, and we set sail from Halifax first thing in the morning —"

George didn't wait for him to finish. "Take me with you," he yelled. "I wanna go!"

Angeline left the steps and knelt in front of George. Taking hold of his hands, she looked into his eyes. "Now, George," she whispered gently, "you know you can't go with us —"

"Why not?" exclaimed George. "I'll be good — I promise!"

Angeline glanced back at Joseph, who looked on helplessly. Angeline turned back to George. She placed her hands gently upon his shoulders and said softly, "Look, baby, we can't take you with us. Besides … this is your home —"

George pushed Angeline's hands away. "This ain't my home!"

Tears started to run down the boy's cheeks. Angeline reached up to dry them, but George stepped away. She sighed and folded her hands into her lap. Joseph looked on in silence.

Angeline sighed again and said, "I'm so sorry, George — next time maybe you can come with us —"

"Ain't nobody wants me. Nobody!" George yelled, fleeing from the yard.

George aimlessly wandered the shoreline until, as dusk began to set in, he found himself again near the path that led to the slaughterhouse. He followed it through the brush and into the clearing below. From the slaughterhouse, George could see a throng of workers hauling carts full of barrels down to the dock. George followed them down, staying in the shadows. For some time he watched them work. Eventually, a man standing on the brig began yelling orders and the workers started filing onto the cargo ship. By this time night had fully set in, and in all the commotion they didn't see that a boy had slipped onboard behind them.

3

In Search of Home

> Home is not where we live, it is where we belong.
>
> —AFRICAN PROVERB

God only knows how George managed to survive the three-day journey across the ocean undetected. He stayed hidden in the dark hull below, tossed to and fro by the relentless swaying of the ship, and surrounded by the endless groaning of the keel as it crashed against the gigantic waves of the Atlantic Ocean. And, of course, George would have had absolutely no clue where or when the ship would ever come ashore. This, to say the least, could have ended a lot worse for the young boy.

But survive he did. The groaning and shuddering finally came to an end. The big cargo door high above was abruptly thrown open to reveal a clear bright sky. As he dashed up the ladder, his lungs gasping at the fresh air, George was greeted by an astonished crew of sailors clamouring about the deck. Like any young boy caught in a place where he shouldn't be, he instinctively ran as fast he could. Scurrying down the long plank to the dock, he disappeared into the crowd along the pier before anyone put together what had happened.

It turns out, he had landed in Boston. This was the gateway to the Americas, built at the rise of the Atlantic trade to the New World. Five-storied warehouses extended almost half a mile into the sea atop massive wharfs. Giant ships filled the harbour. As far as his eyes could see, there were soaring sail masts and enormous smokestacks of transatlantic steamers lining the waters. Turning around he saw, to his amazement, railway trains coasting high in the air along tracks elevated on massive shimmering steel pillars. Wagons crisscrossed underneath, veering down wide avenues. Majestic buildings, with brass trimmings glittering in the sunlight, stood on either side.

And so many white people! As they streamed past him, he marvelled at the extravagance of their clothing. Women were draped in bell-shaped dresses decorated in lace that floated just above the pavement, while on their heads sat wide hats with lavish garlands of flowers flowing over. The men sported impressive top hats and crisp three-piece suits with silky ties tucked in, along with shiny black shoes. Even the coloured folk passing by were decked in remarkably handsome clothing, at least compared to those from the humble settlement of Africville.

Lost in the spectacle of this new world, George continued to wander down this grand avenue. Eventually, he came upon a smaller wharf where several ferries were docked. Standing at the bottom of the plank beside the first ferry, he noticed a man in a long dark suit and hard cap helping passengers disembark. Flashing in the sun were bright silver buttons on the cuffs of his jacket. George fought through the oncoming crowd of people making their way from the ship. Finally, he approached the man in the suit from behind and grabbed his arm.

"Joseph," he yelled excitedly, "it's me, George!"

The man turned and gave a curious look at the boy pulling on his sleeve.

George immediately stepped back. "You're not Joseph," he exclaimed. "Why are you wearing his suit?"

The man took a long hard look at the boy. "As for the suit, young man, this one's mine. And as for Joseph, I reckon he's at home enjoying his leave from work …"

"Well, I need to see him," George pleaded.

"He'll be back here in two days' time." The porter peered closer. "What did you say your name was, son?"

"George," he quietly repeated.

"Okay — George — I'll let him know you were asking. In the meantime, you better get back to your folks …"

At this the porter began to scan the line of people. Before he could turn his attention back to the boy, George had vanished into the crowd.

He continued to wander the streets for the rest of the day, until wagons began to pull back to the warehouses, and people climbed the stairs to the elevated platforms and disappeared into the trains leaving downtown. George began rummaging through odd boxes left by vendors. Finding a handful of fruit, he left the main avenue for a quieter alley and sat down behind a stoop under a small doorway. As he finished eating his spoils, George leaned his head against the wall. Before long, he closed his eyes and fell asleep.

Several days later, George was crouched behind a wagon propped on the edge of the main street along the Boston Harbor. He was peering intently through the crowd at a cart of fruit in the distance. When the coast was clear, he dashed toward the cart. He snatched a handful of apples and turned to run. Unfortunately, George tripped as he tried to jump between two people passing by and sprawled onto the ground.

The vendor spun around. Seeing the boy he yelled, "You little varmint!"

He shook his clenched fist at George and started toward him. For a second George froze. Then he clambered to his

Boston Harbor, 1901.

feet and fled into the crowd. He danced around people heading in every direction. George looked over his shoulder to see whether the man was still chasing him and ran right into a person standing in the crowd. Hands reached out to grab him as he fell backwards. Looking up, George was surprised to see who was staring back at him.

"George!" Angeline exclaimed, wrapping her arms around him. Letting out a deep sigh she said, "Thank God, I've been looking all over for you!"

It was some days before Angeline and Joseph could find the time to return to Africville. Angeline had already sent a letter ahead to Ethel, explaining all that happened. The porter whom George had mistaken for Joseph turned out to have a wife who hired Angeline on occasion to fix her dresses. Shortly after her husband's encounter with George, she had made a point of sharing this strange tale with Angeline, recalling that a boy fitting George's description was desperate to find Joseph. Angeline and Joseph had been scouring the city streets in the hope of finding the boy before something terrible happened to him. And, by sheer luck, George had literally run into her down by the harbour. Soon, Angeline wrote, they would be on their way to Ethel's house with the boy.

George's adventure in Boston had come to an end. As Joseph pulled the wagon up to the Dixon house back in Africville, Ethel appeared outside the front door. Angeline quickly jumped off to greet her. Joseph led George around to the back porch, where the two of them sat quietly as the women talked. After a long while, the back door opened. George looked over to see Ethel walking across the porch toward him. He quickly jumped up and hugged her. For a long moment they stood with arms wrapped tightly around each other. Finally, Ethel squeezed his hand and led him into the house. As they passed Angeline and Joseph, the two of them gave George a hug and assured him they'd take him down to the ocean the next day before they returned home.

Life, initially, was fairly peaceful back in Africville. Josiah had left on a delivery route quite far into New Brunswick.

George spent his days with Ethel, helping with chores where he could, sitting on the porch, and spending afternoons down at the water or up the ridge picking berries. On occasion, Ethel and George attended the worship service at Seaview Baptist Church. After the services, they often took walks down to the ocean shore and collected pebbles. It was early autumn in these days, and life was good in Africville.

But a few weeks later, Josiah came home. On the first night of his return, George was left alone in the living room while Josiah and Ethel talked in their bedroom, their voices ebbing back and forth between shouting and whispers. George had fallen asleep on the couch, and was woken early the next morning by Josiah marching out the front door and slamming it behind him. It was late the next evening before he came by the house again. No one said a word to each other for a few days. Eventually, as the days went by, people seemed content to move on with George being part of the house.

A couple of months later, they were sitting in the living room when they heard a knock at the front door. Josiah left the room to answer it.

"Hello, can I help you?" George heard him say to the stranger.

"I am Mr. A.R. Quinn, of the Canadian census bureau," the man responded. "I am here compiling the profiles of all residents for the 1901 federal census. Are you the head of this household?"

"I am," Josiah slowly replied.

"Then I will need the details of the other members of your household."

Ethel got up and joined Josiah at the door. As the two came to the end of detailing the members of their household, the official noticed George standing just outside the living room.

"And who is this?" he asked.

Ethel and Josiah spun around to see George staring at them. Josiah looked stone faced at the boy.

"And who is this?" the official repeated.

Ethel feigned a smile and turned to Josiah at the door. "Why, our son — of course."

The man stared at Ethel, waiting for her to continue. Finally, he said, "And his name …?"

Ethel blurted, "Yes, I'm sorry — George. George is his name."

"Okay then …" The man looked down as he scribbled in his book. "And his date of birth?"

Ethel looked again at the boy, searching for an answer. But George only offered a blank stare.

She turned again and smiled. "Born April — the fifth of April." Ethel took one more feverish glance at George again before continuing, "And he would be six years old … but time does go by so fast, doesn't it?"

The man gave Ethel a strange look, pondering the information before returning to his page.

"Okay," the man mused, "so born on April 5th, 1896. And that would be g-e-o-r-g-e, and last name, d-i-x-s-o-n, correct?"

The man looked at Josiah. Josiah looked at Ethel. They both smiled and nodded.

The official snapped his book shut. "That will be everyone, then?"

Josiah and Ethel again smiled at the official. "Yessir. That's everyone."

The man stepped off the porch and headed back to the road. Josiah closed the door. He stood still, his hand not moving from the latch, silently staring through the windowpane. Ethel looked at George.

She smiled faintly. "Well, I guess you're a Dixson now," she said.

• • •

It takes me a moment to realize that my dad has fallen silent on the other end of the phone. I'm still imagining all the scenes unfolding before me as he starts to chuckle.

"Besides a few pieces your great-aunt Bea threw in for good measure, therein lies the tale of your papa's great escape. I just wish I could say, 'And they lived happily ever after.'"

I stare out the window, still trying to imagine all the details as he described them.

"Yes," I say. "If only that was the ending. From what I recall, Papa disappeared again not long after, didn't he?"

"I'm afraid so," my father confesses. "He was soon jumping box cars on the trains that ran through the settlement, riding from Halifax all the way to Montreal."

"That was common back then, wasn't it?" I ask.

"Yes it was," my father replies. "A whole lotta young men and boys would take the train looking for work — while others just aimed for adventure. Funny enough, Aunt Bea came across an old news clip from the Saint John paper that mentioned a group of boys being caught by police causing mischief along Union Street. Your papa, George, was listed as one of them, along with Seymour Tyler — a real character he was."

"Wait," I interject. "I know that name.... Wasn't he in the battalion marching band with Papa?"

"Sure was," Dad answers. "He became your papa's closest friend, and they remained friends right up until the end. Good ol' Seymour ... your papa's partner in crime from the very start!"

"So what happened to them?" I ask.

"Well," Dad explains, "the police promptly put both George and Seymour into a day school. It was a one-room class on the second floor of the African Methodist Church over on Queen Street in Saint John. Now, one would think that would have been like a prison, but it turned out to be one of the best things that happened to George — 'cause those teachers taught him how to play the cornet! In that little one-room school, son, is where he discovered his love for music."

Dad pauses before continuing. "It's too bad they closed that school down — maybe life would have been different for those boys ..."

It's hard to imagine that it all started from such humble beginnings. Perhaps this is the significance of Papa's story, that it is not where he finished in life, but how far he had to walk in life to get anywhere at all.

"What happened to them after that?" I ask.

"George had no plans to go back to Africville, that much was certain. Instead, he jumped on a schooner and travelled around the world!"

I hear Dad chuckling again. "And to think, he hadn't even reached his eleventh birthday."

"Are you kidding?" I exclaim. "Man, our grandfather was persistent as a boy, I'll give him that. I'm surprised he ever came back ..."

"Well," my dad says, "on the surface it sounds like a great life for a boy. Your papa certainly tried to make the most of it — he was gone for close to three years. The sea offered George the feeling of freedom. But in the end, son, it can also be a terribly lonely place."

It's getting late, and I can hear the weariness in his voice as my dad says, "As for me, it's time to stretch my legs. Will you give me a call later, son?"

It's hard for me to leave the conversation with more questions than answers but I let him go, assuring him I'll call again very soon.

4

Black in Indiantown

The systems are made to disenfranchise us, and they're working. We do have opportunities to struggle together, to see each other, to listen to each other, and to fight back together.

—**DESMOND COLE**, activist and author

In the days that follow I try to do more research on the history of my grandfather but discover a rather frustrating problem. On every census, there was this persistent practice of the family names being spelled differently. Josiah and Ethel had a different spelling of their last name on every census taken from 1871 to 1911. It would shift from "Dickson" to "Dixson," then to "Dicson," along with the occasional "Dixon," and back again. Of course, this wasn't unusual at that time, for many in the coloured communities were not literate, and often they were content to let the official who was filling out the census write it as he pleased. It makes me wonder if there were other Dixons to whom Papa was somehow related. I ask my father what he thinks.

My father ponders this idea for a moment. "Well, as a matter of fact, there was another person, from Papa's early years, who would have shared his last name. Her name was Lena. She was a Dickson — but most everyone knew her by her husband's name. Her husband was John O'Ree, a relative of the great Willie O'Ree from Fredericton, who became the first Black professional hockey player in the NHL. He was a hero for so many of us young Black kids growing up in our time.

"But make no mistake, Lena O'Ree became a legend in her own right as well, a real force in our community. You see, many kids of colour grew up in a hostile environment, having to face all kinds of hateful treatment and constant bullying, and a lot of us grew to feel either quite bitter toward society, or small and diminished as human beings. Not Lena, though. From a young age, growing up in Indiantown on the north end of Saint John, she had learned a vital lesson. If the fight didn't kill you — it was because you were stronger."

Dad pauses for a moment, I think to make sure that lesson is sinking in, before continuing. "Nothing kept Lena from doing what she put her mind to. In fact, at the young age of seventeen, Lena became the first Black Canadian to host a radio show broadcast across the country. Of course, the station producers kept silent about Lena O'Ree being a woman of colour. That didn't stop Lena from making her voice heard, though. In 1936, a few years after she gained popularity as a radio host, she decided to join the local YWCA. They refused her membership. After she protested, they told Lena she would need five additional Black women to enroll in order to ensure they would socialize on their own in the facility. Lena returned the next day with *ten* Black women."

I can hear Dad laughing in the background as he reminisces on this story. He goes on, "The fact was, nothing could hold Lena back when she put her mind to it. Years later, in 1959, Lena made a decision that would impact Black folk across the country. She took on the cause of having the colour barrier lifted on all the hotels and rail cars owned by the Canadian Pacific company. For generations, Black men had been relegated to working as porters on these rail cars. Now, thanks in large part to Lena, we could ride in passenger seats the same as any other."

As Dad speaks of Lena's incredible achievement, I mentally add her name to the list of other remarkable Black activists throughout Canadian history, some whose names are hardly known, but each one an ancestral giant on whose shoulders we stand. In the '40s, Viola Desmond, a businesswoman from Nova Scotia, refused to leave the whites-only section of a movie theatre, an act of courage that made her a symbol of resistance against segregation. A generation later, Bromley Armstrong, a Jamaican-born labour leader in Ontario, risked his safety by joining "test cases" that exposed landlords and employers who discriminated against Black Canadians, paving the way for stronger human rights protections.

Across the country in British Columbia, Rosemary Brown, who became the first Black woman elected to a Canadian legislature in 1972, used her political voice to fight for gender and racial equality. Born in Halifax but raised in the predominantly Black neighbourhood of Little Burgundy in Montreal, Anthony Sherwood was a talented actor who was blacklisted from the entertainment industry for organizing a Black actors' guild to fight for greater representation in Canadian film and advertisement. He finally broke the colour barrier in Canadian television with his role on the series *Street Legal*. Their stories, along with the tireless work of many others, form a powerful narrative of resilience and determination that has shaped Canada's ongoing journey toward racial justice and equality.

My recollections are interrupted by Dad's voice. "At first, I never understood why your papa showed such disdain for

Lena O'Ree every time her name came up. After all, she did nothing but good for our community. But then I learned the real reason, son." I hear a crackle in Dad's throat as his voice becomes more animated. "It had nothing to do with her! It turns out your grandfather had what I can best describe as a brotherly feud with Lena's *father*, Ernest Dickson."

"Oh," I exclaim, "he had a brother?"

"No ... not exactly. Ernest was the son of George's aunt Cassie — although none in my family, not even Aunt Bea, had any idea how she was related. By the time us children came around, Cassie lived all by herself way up in the north end of Saint John, in Indiantown, and died just a few months before I was born. But there is no doubt that your papa had a close bond to Cassie. In fact, when he signed up for the war, he listed Cassie as his closest kin."

It suddenly occurs to me, "Yes — Cassie Maxwell ... I read that on the attestation paper. I didn't think that name meant anything — until now. With her son being a Dickson, I guess at some point she was also?"

"Who knows?" Dad muses. "As you already found out, Dixon — or Dickson — they were common names back then. I suppose she would have been a relative to your grandfather in some way. He called her "aunt," after all, but I have no clue how it all connects. It's hard to say when George would have first met Cassie, or how he knew where to find her when he stepped off the ship in the Saint John Harbour at the age of fourteen after being gone for the better part of three years. But find her he did …"

I lean back in my chair, and listen as my father's story of the next chapter in George's life unfolds.

• • •

As George disembarked from the ship, he joined the stream of coloured folk making their way past the busy merchant shops, around the social elite chatting idly under the two-storey bandstand in the middle of King's Square, past fancy hotels and the courthouse, and onward to the lower east side of Saint John. Before long, narrow streets were lined with row houses propped against each other. One by one, folk vanished into adjacent doors, until at last he stood by himself at the doorstep of a house.

A moment passed after he knocked, and the door swung open to reveal a middle-aged woman silhouetted by the dim light in the hallway behind her. At first, she cast a suspicious eye at George as he stood just off the edge of the darkened street. As she peered more closely, a shocked expression came over her face. Then her face softened, and a wry smile appeared.

"Well," she chuckled, "you were the last person I expected to see in one piece. Well, c'mon in." The woman beckoned him through the door. "You must be hungry."

After chatting over a plate of food, the lady took a long hard look at the young man sitting across from her.

"Hmm, I'd say you talk like a gentleman now," Cassie said with a wink. "Yet you still stand no taller than a boy. So, which are ya?"

George momentarily looked away in embarrassment, then abruptly straightened his shoulders. "I'm a gentleman, Aunt Cassie."

The woman smiled again. "So tell me, young sir, how long do you mean to stay in town?"

"Well," George looked to the floor then whispered, "I don't really know …"

Cassie studied George for a moment, then gently responded, "Well, it happens I have an extra room to put you up, till you find your way. I trust you can follow the rules of the house?"

George nodded. "Yes, ma'am."

"All right then," Cassie stated, "and I suppose you won't have any trouble doing a little work around here. I could use an extra set of hands …"

Just then a young man came bounding down the stairs. He appeared to be a few years older than George, dressed out in slacks and a button-down shirt. He stopped in front of the boy as he reached for his jacket on the hook. At first he barely glanced at George, then paused long enough to notice who it was.

As he threw on his jacket he quipped, "So, you're back."

"Now, Ernest," Cassie replied with a slight irritation in her voice, "that is hardly a way to welcome George back. George, you remember Ernest, my son? Anyway, I suppose you'll both have time to get reacquainted. George is gonna stay with us for a little while. I'll put him up in the laundry room."

Cassie turned her nose down to the older boy. "He's also willing to provide some much-needed help."

Ernest ignored her mother's comments as he turned toward the door.

"Well, he better not go into my room," he flatly retorted. "I'll be back later, I'm just gonna see Jessie."

"Figures," Cassie muttered. "I hardly see you now that Jessie caught your attention."

The young man called back as he disappeared out the door, "Gotta make the best of the time I have before I leave on the next rail car, Mama. See you!"

As the door closed behind him, Cassie sighed and turned her attention back to George, "Don't mind Ernest. Like you, he grew up too fast. C'mon, let's get you settled in."

George soon realized Cassie indeed had need of his help. In the room where George stayed there were piles of laundry that Cassie had collected from hotels and wealthy homeowners, all of which were overdue to be returned. She put George to work hauling the bags to the back porch, then scrubbing and rinsing while Cassie hung them to dry before bringing them onto the dining room table to iron flat. True to his word, Ernest left to work on the railway not long after George arrived. Side by side, George and Cassie worked at making a meagre living. In this moment of their lives, it was evident that both George and Cassie needed one another. Little did they know how much their relationship would grow in the coming years.

In the months that followed, it became increasingly hard for Cassie to afford to live in the city. Without a husband bringing home wages, Saint John was a tough place for a single Black woman to survive. After the American Revolution, many Black migrants from the States were among the British supporters who settled in the area. Like other Loyalists, they were promised land. However, the plots assigned to them were inadequate to farm — if they were assigned at all. To add insult to injury, Saint John's city charter of 1785 specifically excluded Black people from practising a trade, selling goods, fishing in the harbour, or becoming freemen with a right to vote. These laws stood until 1870.

In short, everything was designed by those with privilege to increase their lot in life, mostly at the expense of others. There were the few exceptions of Black entrepreneurs who managed to find success in the lower end of Saint John. Thomas Washington, for instance, ran a popular restaurant and "hair dressing shop" in Prescott House. He had inherited a large sum of money from his family estate in New Jersey and was able to support his enterprises without any support from white colonial banks and financiers. Most Black people, however, were not as fortunate, and were afforded little opportunity to save enough money to invest in such ventures. Most simply survived on what they earned each passing day, whether it be as a launderer, porter, labourer, or teamster. And not a few, like Cassie, struggled even to put two days of work together. That meant they were ever on the move to find the cheapest places to live.

One morning, George woke up to Cassie and Ernest hollering at each other. From what George gathered, Cassie was trying to get Ernest to help her pack, but her son refused.

"I'm not living out there," Ernest protested.

"Well, we can't afford to live here," cried Cassie.

"*You* can't afford to live here," the young man retorted. "I'll do fine, you'll see."

Standing at the top of the stairs, George watched Cassie's son thunder down the hallway and slam the front door behind him. George ventured down the stairs and peered into the living room to see Cassie stuffing duffle bags with clothing and linen. As George stood at the entrance, he could see tears following the pained lines of her face.

"Well," she said flatly, "are you gonna come with me to Indiantown, or walk out that door like every other man in my life?"

• • •

I sit with the image my father painted of George's touching reunion with Aunt Cassie after years sailing on the ocean, and their close relationship during this season of his young life. George did, of course, go to Indiantown with his aunt Cassie. And, recalling the family stories of life in Indiantown, I am struck how this vibrant life was created by those who lived there, a poignant reminder that the human spirit wills to flourish and find happiness, even when pushed to the margins of society.

Indiantown, as they called it back then, was a place few outside of Saint John would have known even existed. Prior to colonists arriving, it was an important gathering place for the area's Indigenous Peoples, who traded along a bend of the river above the dangerous tides that flowed in from the ocean. By the early seventeenth century, European fur traders had built a permanent trading store nearby, which they called the "Indian House." However, the boom of the industrial era during the eighteenth century changed the way of life along the river dramatically. Settlers began using the river as a natural conduit for shipping products, sending large steam-propelled barges upstream with lumber and goods. The Indian House became overrun with lumber mills, massive boat docks, supply stores, and eventually homes for the increasing number of immigrant families.

In just a short breadth of time, the gathering place of the Indigenous Peoples became a bustling port of foreign goods and European society. And with the beaver supply severely diminished, there was no place for the Indigenous trader in this new world. Indigenous agriculture on the river had been forever changed by the coming of European settlers; all the farmland along the Saint John River had been taken over. After years of being pushed off their traditional territories, by the nineteenth century the Wolastoqiyik had been all but forced onto federal reserve lands.

Meanwhile, life in this fledgling colonial outpost kept going. By the time George found his way there with Cassie, its residents had gained a reputation for living like they were

Main street of Indiantown c. 1900.

still on the frontier. It attracted those who were caught up in the entrepreneurial spirit of the generation past and disdained the establishment class of Saint John. Of course, the ability to turn your nose up at the elite of society is, ironically, contingent upon your own privilege of freedom. Most of the white settlers of Indiantown, as you can imagine, hadn't given much thought to that as Cassie and George trudged up the long main street into town. Racism, unfortunately, lives in the hearts of people, not area codes. Whether folk moved beyond the tracks, or down to the lower end of town, people's view of Black folk didn't change much. Even though Indiantown, on paper, existed outside the charter of Saint John, which explicitly excluded Black people from voting or owning businesses, many of the white folk in Indiantown still treated them as second-class citizens. As a result, a lot of Black families lived a segregated life in Indiantown. Most of them built homes beside each other up on the secluded hill along Spar Cove Road, largely hidden out of sight in the thickly wooded hillside above the bustling town below.

Even for the generation after the world wars, life in Indiantown didn't change a whole lot. My aunt Nornee continued to live there with her husband, Speed, and their children. Their eldest son, my cousin Buncker, still shares his vivid memories of growing up on Spar Cove Road after the Second World War. It was a smaller community by then, with many folk having migrated to the burgeoning cities for work, but he reflects on how life growing up in the north end taught you two things — how to make a meal out of nothing, and how to stick up for one another. Not a day went by when a coloured kid didn't have to fight their way home from school. By virtue of their birthright, older siblings learned to swing fists faster and harder than anyone else. In fact, fighting became so mixed in the blood of our cousins that many left home to make a living in the boxing circuits of New England.

At the same time, Buncker will insist that life in the Black community on Spar Cove Road was full and meaningful. From one end to the other, everyone knew everybody. Boys "ran the road" together, as he affectionally described it, and most every night got into some kind of adventure up in the woods. But most of all, it was the baseball games he remembers. Games on Saturdays brought the community together. They would all gather in the field at the bottom of the road. The game itself would last for hours, and often so far into the night that no one could see the ball. Those weekend ball games on Spar Cove Road were the stuff of legend. Heroes were born on that field, for there was a time when no one along the east coast could play ball better than the boys of Spar Cove.

Back in the late 1800s, Thomas Washington was the main organizer of the first Black baseball clubs in New Brunswick. He would post announcements of games against rival teams.

The Alerts represented Indiantown in the north end, with the Hector brothers being the stars of the team; James (Jumbo) Hector was the pitcher, his brother Charles was the catcher, along with his brother Joe at first base, Oscar at third base, and his youngest brother, George, playing in the right field. Touted as "the strongest colored nines to be found in the maritime provinces," the press noted Jumbo Hector for his graceful curve ball and heavy hitting. Games against rival teams would usually be held at the Barrack Square in the south end of Saint John. As was tradition, games would last until it was too dark to see the ball. The article went on to describe how visiting teams would be dressed in the latest attire, while the boys from Spar Cove would show up with a mixture of long and short trousers, sometimes rolling up pant legs to hide the holes in the knees, and a few players with odd shoes who couldn't afford a matching pair. But the article made a point of mentioning how the folk from Spar Cove Road didn't mind that the crowd snickered at the attire of their young men. By the end of the game, it was them doing the laughing.

My father and I are going back and forth sharing this history, when he interjects.

"Now, getting back to your papa. George, even as a young man, wasn't fast enough to run the bases like the Hector boys or strong enough to fight on the streets. By the way, there was a famous boxer by the same name as your grandfather —"

"Yes — 'Little Chocolate'!" Even our relatives are surprised to learn that our papa and the more famous George Dixon aren't related, even though both are from the north end of Halifax.

"Easy to confuse," my dad agrees. "In fact, Little Chocolate was not much bigger than your grandfather in stature — but boy could he swing those fists. He was probably the greatest fighter that Canada has ever seen. But he was at the height of his boxing career already about the time your grandfather was born."

"Anyway" my dad continues, "none of that mattered to your papa, 'cause he had a love for *music.* To make a name for yourself back then —there was no such thing as YouTube, or TikTok — you literally went onto the street and played in front of anyone passing by. Guys would be busking all hours of the day and night, on street corners and all the way down to the river docks, competing to grab people's attention. There weren't many places for coloured folk to gather, save community halls or church basements, so it meant being creative on the location. For the younger boys, it was often just showing up at the same street corner the next day.

"I can picture him, even now, standing at a busy intersection into the late hours of the night, him and his pal, Seymour. I believe, in my father's last dying days, he imagined heaven would be standing on some street corner past those pearly gates, playing his cornet with a crowd dancing in front of him, and no worry in the world. Yes … that would be heaven for your papa."

I let that image of heaven unfold before me. I am trying to picture my grandfather tapping his feet in rhythm with the song, while the polished brass of his cornet catches the radiance of heavenly light shining around him. A beeping of a call coming on the other line interrupts my thoughts. I reluctantly say goodbye to Dad, but I assure him I will call again soon to hear the next part of the story.

• • •

That evening a lot of questions swirl in my head. Not the least of which is the mysterious figure of Cassie. I decide to see what more I can learn about her, including whether she really was my grandfather's aunt. In his military attestation paper, dated December 1, 1916, George had indeed listed Cassie Maxwell as his next of kin. Upon finding her death certificate, I learn that she died in 1936 as a widow, naming Ernest as her only survivor. It says that her father was David Dixon, and the identity of her mother unknown. I decide to do a quick check on her father to see how far back the records of her lineage go. Eventually, by entering Dickson as an alternate spelling, I find a match to David Dixon, who is listed as having a child by the name of Cassie. The link sends me to a census record, dated 1881. But as I scroll down to her name, the one above catches my attention.

It is listed that David also had a son, named George. It says that George, the elder brother to Cassie, was twenty-three years old at the time of the census, which means he was born around the year 1858. My curiosity is piqued, for I immediately recall that Papa had also listed his father's name as George in a military file unearthed by the retired military friend of my cousin Eunice. I start searching this name in the archival records of the state of Rhode Island. I find only one. It is in a birth registry for children born in the year 1895. Near the top is listed George Richard Dixon, born July 21, 1895, to a father, George W., and a mother, Catherine. It says "George W." was thirty-eight years old — which means he would have been born near the year 1858.

I keep staring at my computer screen. I wonder, am I missing something? Am I really staring at the secret to my grandfather's parents? In the moment, it seems incredible that my grandfather was hiding the answer to his past in plain sight. However, as a teacher, how many times did I tell students to let the evidence guide them to the most plausible answer to their questions? There appears little reason to doubt this was the true record of my grandfather's birth.

As I search further, I can't find any record of when my grandfather's father passed away, and whether he ever ventured to see his son again. His name appears only once more, years later in a Pawtucket, Rhode Island, housing directory, dated about the time George left for the war. Perhaps, somehow, George had connected with him in that brief moment when he resurfaced, explaining why he mentioned his father still being alive. As for his mother, Catherine, I could find absolutely no evidence of her existence beyond this single reference. It is safe to presume, like George alluded to in his military file, that her life on this earth was brief and most likely troubled. Either way, whatever George knew of his parents, he chose to hide both of them in the past.

• • •

The next day, I call my father and share every detail I found.

For a while, he remains silent. Then I hear him whisper softly, as if to himself, "Why must I learn this now? Everyone, my brothers and sisters, all gone. I'm the only one to hear this. Perhaps in heaven I can tell them …"

My heart aches for him.

He breathes a long sigh before saying, "On that note, some may never know, 'cause I suspect a few of them are stuck in a place I have no intention of going to! Maybe the Lord could send a message through Lazarus, but I ain't planning to join them!"

The emotional weight of the moment lifts, and I join my dad in laughter.

"Thank you, son, for sharing this with me. It does help make sense of a lot of things, doesn't it? I always wondered about Cassie. But back then life was, well, chaotic, and I never really thought to make sense of it. In those days, we mostly accepted things as they were told to us and moved on. I suppose there's so much more to the story, but you've revealed much more than what I expected to learn in my lifetime. Thank you."

I'm moved by my dad's response. "Well, I would not have arrived at this without the help of Eunice's friend, so we're all indebted. It was meant to be that you should hear it now. I guess that's all that needs to be said."

5

Band of Brothers

God has wrought many things out of oppression.
He has endowed his creatures with the capacity to create,
and from this capacity has flowed the sweet songs of
sorrow and joy that have allowed man to cope with his
environment and many different situations.

—REV. DR. MARTIN LUTHER KING JR., address
to the Berlin International Jazz Festival

A few weeks later, I'm finally able to take an extra day off work and visit my dad in Regina over the Thanksgiving weekend. I must confess, after the first time experiencing the vast flatlands of the prairies, driving across it becomes a tedious exercise of staying awake. But it is important for me to see him, so I jump in the car and head off.

The next morning, we settle into his living room. As he gets comfortable in his chair, I casually look around and notice the photo of my grandfather with the battalion marching band on the hutch against the wall. For as long as I can remember, my father has always kept a copy of the photo somewhere on display. It is now a familiar image, my grandfather

Members of the No. 2 marching band: (*back row*) Albert Carty, Fred Charles Dixon, Percy William Thomas, and James Albert Sadlier; (*front row*) Herbert Nichols, George Richard Dixon, Band Master Sergeant George William Stewart, Arthur Seymour Tyler, and Harold Bushfan.

sitting cross-legged on the ground between his fellow band members, all dressed in uniform with their instruments in hand, staring resolutely into the camera. And yet, the story of the band itself is something I know little about. It remains a far-off moment frozen in time. I carry the photo over and set it down across from my father.

"Dad, did you ever hear Papa play his cornet?"

As he glances at the photo, a sadness comes over his face. "No, son, I never did. I used to beg your nana for music lessons. I wanted to learn how to play the piano. Finally, after the hundredth time pleading and pulling on her apron, she turned to me and said in a tone that took me aback, 'Son, we can't afford it — it's as simple as that.'"

My dad continues, "And then I discovered your papa's cornet in the closet. As far as I recall, I never once saw him take it out, and I suspect it stayed there right up until the night —"

At this moment my dad seems to be interrupted by another memory. I'm about to ask what's on his mind, but he presses on with the story. "There were moments, as a boy, I'd peek into the closet, tempted to play it. I figured, just one time at least. My mama would catch me and sternly tell me to keep the door closed. I quickly learned that it was something not to touch or speak of. There was something about that cornet that Papa preferred to keep hidden in the dark."

"And yet," I comment, "he never parted with it."

The sadness deepens over my father's face.

"No, he never parted with it. There were memories attached to that cornet he couldn't let go of, I suppose, no matter how painful. In the end, I'm afraid the weight of those memories became a burden all of us carried in some way or another."

I'm getting the sense this topic is raising difficult memories for my father. But at the same time, I'm intrigued by my grandfather's complicated relationship with his cornet.

"Dad, I get why Papa would want to be part of a band — but why a band going to war? I suspect he really didn't want to be a part of it, did he?"

"You're right," Dad replies. "In those brief years leading up to the war, George was enjoying what were possibly the best years of his life. He had friendship and music to fill his days and, thanks to Aunt Cassie, a home where he could peacefully rest his head at night. I like to think your grandfather was finally becoming content with life."

I see Dad drifting again, as if holding his father in that special place and time. Shaking his head, he presses on. "Of course, when Canada first entered the war in 1914, George's life hardly changed. No one came looking for him and his friends to join. In fact, the few Black men who ventured to sign up when the war started were sent back with the clear message that it was a 'white man's war.' And so, for a time life carried on as normal. But, as we know, the war started taking a terrible toll on soldiers fighting overseas."

Over the course of our conversation, Dad and I piece together the circumstances that surrounded George at this point in his life. It's well known how brutal the fighting was during the First World War. Western militaries were unprepared for the scale of carnage inflicted by modern weapons of war. For instance, during the second battle of Ypres, on the western border of Belgium, over a third of the 18,000 Canadian soldiers who fought there were killed or injured in the first forty-eight hours of engagement. It is notoriously remembered for the first large-scale use of poison gas by the German army. By the end of the month-long battle, over 105,000 casualties were suffered among the Allied troops.

Meanwhile, back in Canada there were a growing number of Black men who felt it was their place to fight in the Great War, and these desperate circumstances finally seemed their moment of opportunity to be accepted into the ranks. But they would have to overcome two hurdles if they were going to achieve their goal. First, despite the circumstances, military generals still refused to entertain the inclusion of Black soldiers among the ranks of white soldiers. But they were desperate, so the generals reluctantly offered conditions for men of colour to join the military. For Black men to serve, they needed to form their own battalion and — since no Black officer existed in the military — they would need to convince a white officer to leave his post and assume command of these coloured men.

However, racism ran so deep within the military brass that it seemed improbable any white commissioned officer would sacrifice his career to lead an untrained Black battalion into war. But such a man did emerge. His name was Daniel Hugh Sutherland. People say he was a religious man who, growing up in River John, a rural area in Pictou County, Nova Scotia, carried a down-to-earth approach to life and had an understanding of our folk that few other white men possessed. Sutherland not only had a heart for the cause of our people, he was as smart as they come. He was an engineer by trade, having built bridges, dams, and railroads across Canada.

Sutherland had just begun his military career when he heard the call from higher ranks that they were looking for an officer to lead a battalion made up of coloured men — not for battle, but for construction, for the military brass still did not trust these men to fight. Sutherland showed little regard for skin colour as he took the challenge of his first command. It was about taking willing men to go to the front lines and serve. In Sutherland, the men found a leader under whom they could finally rally a battalion for the battle, or so they thought.

That, however, led to the second hurdle they needed to overcome. The government had created a real problem in refusing men of colour at the beginning of the war. Why, in

Recruitment sign for the No. 2 Construction Battalion posted by the Canadian military.

their most desperate hour of need, did they now think Black men would suddenly be eager to join? The bitterness of being treated so unjustly in the early months of the war ran deep and was not easily forgiven. Besides, many men of colour took exception to being segregated on the battlefield. They predicted they would just become fodder on the front lines, without any support from the white soldiers.

After the No. 2 Construction Battalion was sent overseas in March 1917, Black men who objected to the war were forced into duty by a military conscription imposed in the summer of 1917, upon "all men in British lands." Incensed at this bitter irony, many men of colour refused. This led to the police pulling Black men off the streets and demanding to see their exemption papers. Few had any, which meant they were dragged over to the military recruitment office. Of course, when they arrived, the Canadian military had a policy of segregated regiments — which created a dilemma to say the least! Quite a few ended up filling fatigue and labour duties. Other unwilling participants were sent off to join the men of the segregated No. 2 Construction Battalion already stationed on the eastern front in France.

In the early days of assembling the battalion, men who did want to fight were straggling into Truro from various regions across the country. Sutherland must have realized the dilemma of relying on the government to gather enough men of colour to form a full battalion. So, he started to come up with another idea to recruit soldiers. His plan was to create a sense of pride and dignity in being part of the first Black battalion to ever serve the nation. In those days, the best way to raise the spirit of folks was to, well, strike up a parade! But to have a parade, Sutherland needed a band.

• • •

As we arrive at this point in history, my father leans over the arm of his chair, his hand moving about quite excitedly. "And that, my son, is how a ragtag group of musicians from the streets of Saint John found themselves at the centre of this story!"

"Do you remember the guys he played with?" I ask.

Dad picks up the picture of the band members and studies their faces. "Sure I do." He begins to point them out, one by one. "First, there was Herbert Nichols, who lived two doors down from your papa in Indiantown. They were real close and hung out every chance they could wherever music was happening — on street corners and dance halls, it didn't matter! They were lucky to have grown up at a time when some of the best musicians on the whole east coast came right from the north end of Saint John.

"There was the leader of the band, George William Stewart. George William was just a few years older than George and Herbert, but he was the kind of no-nonsense, take-charge character that made him a natural leader. Yes, good ol' George William, a cooper by day and a bandmaster by night. He had a swagger that made him something of a lady's man.

"And then there was Harold Bushfan, whose cousin I think was married to George William at the time. But what I do remember is that he had a great sense of humour. And then there was James Sadlier, and his younger brother-in-law, Percy Thomas. Both of them were the sweetest men you ever met. And there were a couple of older chaps who were already playing with George William before your papa, the younger George, came on the scene. One was Fred, who also went by the last name of Dixon, but there was no connection to each other beyond that, at least as far as anyone knew. And the other was Albert Carty, who had grown up in the West Indies. What brought Albert to Saint John, New Brunswick — your guess would be as good as mine.

And finally, there was Seymour — what a wonderful character he was! His older sister was married to Albert Carty. I think Albert only put up with him because of that. From all accounts, Seymour was a talented musician — when he wasn't recovering from some fall or ailment. Which made him the most unlikely of the group to become preoccupied with enlisting as a soldier in the war. And yet he made every effort to do so! God bless him, soon after the Great War broke out, Seymour tried to join the 104th Battalion being raised out of Sussex, New Brunswick. He, along with eighteen other coloured men, showed up to get enlisted. Little did they know that letters had already been circulating in the military that men of colour were a liability for war and not to be recruited. All nineteen were sent home by the commander, Lieutenant Colonel Fowler, for no other reason than having the wrong colour of skin.

"But that didn't discourage Seymour from trying again. He was either too stubborn, stupid, or saintly to see prejudice as a barrier to serving his country. When news of an all-Black battalion surfaced many months later, Seymour was the first one interested in joining. How he managed to convince your papa and the others to enlist is a tale often retold …"

• • •

Seymour bounded down the basement stairs of the African Methodist Episcopal Church to where a band of his brothers, talented young men from the streets of Saint John who played brass instruments, often practised. Waving a newspaper wildly in his hands, he interrupted the music.

"Boys!" he yelled. "Did you hear the news? They finally allowing us coloured men to join!"

The band members paused and looked over at Seymour with a mix of sceptical and bewildered looks. Seymour flipped open the paper and begin to read, albeit rather poorly given his lack of schooling.

"The Coloured Man's own … Battalion under … Lt. Col. D.H. … Sutherland."

The musicians were quickly becoming impatient. Undeterred, Seymour kept reading.

"Enlist today and prove your … gratitude for the … precious … heritage … of freedom found only in the British empire."

A few men start scoffing and chuckling. Seymour scowled at them over the top of the paper, but kept reading.

"This is a … construction … battalion … that is badly needed —"

Some now broke out in laughter. Seymour was clearly not amused, and tried with greater earnestness to read, while now prodding at the paper.

"It is now more … important than a fighting … battalion, because bridges and roads must be rebuilt to keep the fighting men supplied —"

Now the group laughed in unison, while some threw up their hands. Seymour had had enough.

"Why you laughing?!"

Noticing his clear displeasure with the group, George William took it upon himself to walk over and reason with poor Seymour.

"First off," George William gently began, "You really think they gonna take you, Seymour? They already rejected you. You tried to join the other battalion, and they just turned you around — for no other reason than you were coloured." He paused to let that sink in. "Has the colour of your skin changed since then?"

Seymour pressed his finger into the paper again. "But it says right here this battalion is for coloured men … our very own —"

Now it was Fred's turn to intervene. "But not for fighting — they just gonna put us on the front lines to work. No glory in that …"

Seymour hesitated. "Well sure … maybe at first — but we won't stay there for long. We just need to prove ourselves, is all." He paused for a second, then lifted his chest. "You don't think we have what it takes to fight?"

The musicians looked at one other, pondering the question. Eventually, Albert approached Seymour, with a concerned look on his face.

"Look, Seymour," he said gently. "Fighting takes a toll on the strongest of men. I'd be lyin' if I didn't admit that your sister and me … well, you get sick easily and …"

Seymour stepped away. "I don't need you making excuses for me." He folded the paper under his arm and stormed up the stairs. The others were left looking at one another with varied expressions across their faces.

A few days later, Seymour again came running in with a newspaper.

"Boys!" Seymour yelled, as groans from the other men filled the basement room.

"Let me guess," Fred quipped, "they now recruiting coloured men to shine the general's shoes!"

The others roared with laughter. This time Seymour ignored them.

"Nope. A new ad just came out, and it says here that the … commander of the coloured battalion … Lt. Col. … Sutherland, is looking to form a marching band to help raise morale for the cause of our very own battalion!"

The musicians fell quiet. Some curiously glanced over at Seymour. Buoyed by the attention they were now affording him, Seymour enthusiastically shouted, "C'mon boys, this is our moment!" He turned to George William and pleaded, "After all, what better band is there on the east coast? We could drum up support in no time!"

While George William pondered Seymour's words, the others glanced anxiously at one another. Once again, Fred spoke up. "I don't know, Seymour, I got a wife and kids to take care of ..." This prompted nods and mutters from the older musicians.

But Seymour would not relent. "What are we going to be in this world? How many moments like this will come to us in our lifetime? Do you think this war has nothing to do with us?"

Seymour seemed to arrive at a moment of great conviction. He stood in the midst of them, looked them in the eyes, and spoke with an eloquence that surprised everyone present.

"You boys realize we ain't really free here — you do know that, right? Someday we will know what freedom truly is, because we fought for it. And we'll be remembered as heroes, remembered for courage and bravery. But nothin' will ever change if we stay here in this basement. Boys, I don't know much, but this I'm sure of — we ain't free until we fight to be free."

At that, Seymour turned and resolutely walked up the stairs, leaving the others in complete silence.

The following night, Herbert and George were walking the long road back to Indiantown from the city. They were unusually quiet. Eventually, Herbert spoke up. "George, what d'ya think of Seymour's sermon yesterday? Ya know, about being the marching band for the troops?"

George kept staring down at the road. "I dunno. Haven't much thought about it since then."

Herbert hesitated for a moment then said, "Well, I was thinking we should join. I dunno if I can stay here my whole life, travellin' up and down this road, playin' our music to the same folk every night. We could be famous, George, what d'ya think about that?"

George's eyes didn't leave the road. "I dunno. I been across the ocean, and nothin' I found there makes me wanna go back."

Herbert turned his attention to the road again, and together they walked silently home, each man lost in his own thoughts on the war.

A few days later, in August of 1916, Herbert, Harold, and Percy walked into the basement where the other band members were setting up for rehearsal. They stopped just inside the doorway.

Herbert coughed and cleared his throat. "Boys ..." he slowly began, "we got to thinking about what Seymour said.... He's right. Brothers, this may be our one chance to make a name for ourselves. At least we owe it to ourselves to try ..."

The other men sat in stunned silence.

Herbert turned to Seymour. "So count us in, we'll join you."

Seymour sprung toward Herbert and hugged him, then he threw his arms around Harold and Percy. Herbert walked over to where George sat with a sullen face and eyes fixed to the floor. Herbert reached his hand toward George, but his friend didn't move. Meanwhile, the older men worked their way around the room, shaking the hands of the four younger members and muttering words of encouragement.

By the following week, the four of them had boarded the train to Truro, Nova Scotia, to join the other recruits of the No. 2 Construction Battalion. All except Seymour, that is. The poor soul got sick on the way, so they had to send him to a military hospital in Pictou! It was a month before he finally joined his friends at training camp.

Back in Saint John, the rest of the band attempted to carry on. They showed up for rehearsal, tried to fill in the music as best they could, but performing just wasn't the same. The shadow of the war across the ocean was now hanging over them as well. Every day that they walked into the rehearsal room, the empty stools where their friends once sat were a stark reminder of how different the world had become. A few more weeks went by. One morning, George walked downstairs into a hushed room. Albert, George William, James, and Fred were quietly packing their instruments.

A confused and desperate look came over George's face. "Hey — what y'all doing?"

George William turned and looked at the younger George.

"I ain't a soldier, George," he declared. "But I'm a man who's got pride. Seymour's right, we got no more certainties about life standin' here than on the battlefield. And he's also right that we happen to be the best damn band on the east coast." The others nodded. "If this be our time, well, we figured we oughta make the best of the time we been given."

George William stepped toward their younger friend. "C'mon George, why don't you join us?"

The younger George stared silently at the floor. One by one, the older men filed past him, each patting him on the back as a parting gesture. George William was the last to say goodbye.

"See you, George. Take good care of yourself."

More weeks passed. George resigned himself to wandering the streets. A few times he tried playing on his own, but the music sounded muted and lonely. As the cold winter days of December approached, the wind sweeping across the streets left George feeling the bitterness of being alone. One afternoon, while Cassie was preparing dinner, she was surprised by the sound of the front door bursting open. An instant later George appeared at the kitchen doorway.

"Aunt Cassie," George shouted as he excitedly waved papers in the air. "I did it — I'm gonna join my friends in the marching band!"

Shock came over Cassie's face. George began laying the papers on the kitchen table. He didn't notice Ernest standing behind him, listening intently to what the commotion was about.

George scanned the papers, then turned to Cassie and said, "Only problem is, I need you to help me sign these papers the officer gave me —"

Ernest interrupted him. "What? Ain't no way you gettin' my ma to sign anything over to the war brass. First thing that goes wrong, they're comin' for my ma. Besides, the war ain't for folk like us. White folk made that clear — they don't even care about you."

George spun around. "Speak for yourself, Ernest! I ain't goin' to war for no white man. I wanna go because my friends are there! They care about me — which is more than what anyone can say about you!"

Ernest clenched his fist. "Why, you son of a —"

Before he finished the sentence, Ernest had swung at George. George ducked. Ernest lunged at George, sending both of them into the kitchen table. Cassie screamed at the two boys to stop. But Ernest ignored her. He pinned the smaller George to the floor and starting punching him. Cassie ran over, grabbing at her son's arm. Finally, Ernest relented. Cassie stooped to help George off the floor, who was gasping in pain.

Ernest, breathing heavily, pointed his finger at George, "Look at you — you can't even stand up for yourself in my ma's kitchen, how you possibly going to survive a day on a battlefield?! They'll just throw your life away, George, 'cause it don't mean nothin' to them."

He let out another deep breath before continuing, "None of us mean much at all to them. Find a battle at least worth fightin' for — but for God's sake, leave my ma out of it."

He turned and stormed out of the room. As George lay on the floor, his eyes welled up with tears. Cassie tried consoling him, but he pushed himself away. Wiping back the tears, he stumbled to his feet and left the kitchen. Cassie stood alone as she heard the front door slam behind him.

A couple of days later, Cassie heard the front door slowly creak open. She peered from the kitchen to see George stepping inside and anxiously looking around.

"C'mon in," Cassie gently called down the hallway. "You must be hungry."

As Cassie turned back to her cooking, George quietly slipped into a chair at the kitchen table.

"Don't worry," Cassie said. "Ernest headed out looking for work yesterday. I expect he'll be gone for a few weeks."

She took a bowl from the cupboard, scooped some soup from the pot, and placed it in front of George. It didn't take long for George to finish the bowl. Cassie served him more soup. As George was finishing, Cassie cautiously began to speak. "George, I'm sorry about Ernest, he means well. These days, it's hard for any of us to figure out what's right in life.

I've seen you grow into a young man since you come into my home. I don't know all you went through before coming here, but it's clear where you need to be."

Cassie let out a long, deep sigh. "Men come and go in my life. I wish you would stay. But Lord knows I won't be the one to keep another from a life beyond this place. If joining the marching band with your friends is where you need to be, then I'll be happy to sign those papers for you."

George raised his eyes from the table. "You done so much for me, Aunt Cassie. I'll never forget it."

"You better not," Cassie chuckled. "Lord knows too many men have left me without a thought afterward — I'd like to think one man in this world can hold a fond memory of Cassie Maxwell!"

6

The Will to Fight

Then distress fell on the nation,
And the flag was drooping low;
Should the dust pollute your banner?
No! the nation shouted, No!
So when War, in savage triumph,
Spread abroad his funeral pall—
Then you called the colored soldiers,
And they answered to your call.

— PAUL LAURENCE DUNBAR,
"The Colored Soldiers"

The next morning, I make my way to the kitchen, brew a cup of coffee, then sit in the living room as I wait for my father to appear from his sleep. It's a welcome moment of solitude, as I don't feel quite ready to move on from what my dad and I shared the day before. I start thinking again about the circumstances in which my grandfather and his generation lived at the time the war began, and I wonder what I would have done had I been in their shoes. I'm grateful for not needing to face such decisions. My early morning reflection is interrupted by my dad shuffling down the hallway.

After breakfast together, I help him get settled into his chair. The weather has turned, and a light rain has begun to fall. Just as well, I say to myself, for I am hoping my father and I will spend most of the day in more conversation. I begin by asking his thoughts on what I was pondering earlier.

"You know, Dad, I was thinking about all that transpired between George and the other men around him leading up to the war. There were a lot of conflicting views about the war in the Black community at the time, weren't there?"

My dad takes a moment to think about this.

"Well," he begins, "you need to understand those were very difficult times. Before the turn of the last century, us Black folk were so small in number in this country that white folk hardly thought of our existence, save for when we showed up in the morning to clean their clothes and fix their barn doors. But the Jim Crow segregation laws down south made life so oppressive for Black folk, they were desperate to get out. And many Canadians became quite nervous as more Black migrants started crossing the border.

"Yes," I comment, "the whole anti-Black immigration sentiment that spread in the late 1800s is well documented."

"It wasn't just sentiment," Dad replies. "Many of us were shut out of jobs, sent to sparse and remote places across the country, and children were pushed into segregated schools in urban neighbourhoods. And yet, more from the south kept coming. Eventually, the government shut the borders to Black folk. In so many ways, we were on our own up here."

As my father pauses, I see the familiar look he gave his congregation when he was particularly serious about his point. I nod to let him know it wasn't lost on me. He then continues. "As far as many were concerned, the war was another threat to our survival as Black folk in this country. As for your papa, while he held a grudge against his cousin Ernest for personal reasons, I can't say I hold a grudge against Ernest for his views. You ought to read some of the archived telegrams the military generals sent back and forth to each other, then you can see for yourself the outright prejudice they held against us. It's a shame really, that it's taken this country a hundred years to recognize how poorly our people were treated."

My father's words, truly, are not lost on me. In light of the systemic racism and discrimination they faced over the generations, it is remarkable that any of them were still willing to sacrifice their lives for a society that scorned them. I suppose they were motivated for different reasons, but nevertheless, I am not sure I would have been able to embrace such selfless service in those circumstances. Even with the privilege I have gained, thanks to the sacrifice of those who came before me, I have never thought of risking my life to protect this country. Which brings to the forefront of my mind the ones who did.

"So," I remark, "when the men finally did assemble on the fields of Truro to form the No. 2 Construction Battalion, I am sure they were motivated to prove society wrong."

"Well, Lieutenant Colonel Sutherland was certainly motivated," my dad responds. "It didn't take him long to bring together this fledgling band of musicians and put them to work. Even in the winter days of December, Sutherland organized parades down the main streets of any village or town where Black folk happened to live. George proudly marched in step with his fellow musicians, trumpeting songs that evoked shouts of certain victory on the battlefield. On real cold days they huddled on stages in the basements of churches and community halls, filling the room with big band music, stirring enthusiasm among young recruits as they swung on the dance floor in time with their dance partners.

"And on the days when the sun warmed the winter afternoons, Lieutenant Colonel Sutherland had them perform on bandstands in open parks under blue skies. Wherever and whenever he could muster a crowd, Lieutenant Colonel Sutherland had the marching band play. He was determined

Members of the No. 2 Construction Battalion with Lt. Col. Daniel Hugh Sutherland and other officers.

to pull together enough men to be considered a strong enough battalion that would make a difference in the war raging overseas.

"But it wasn't easy. As much as Sutherland wanted to prove their worth, in fairness most of the men who showed up had no skills whatsoever to fight on the battlefield. And with men straggling in from all over the country, they hardly knew one another. And, of course, they had to accomplish the impossible in the face of social expectations that they would fail. No, training in Truro turned out to be no easy picnic for Sutherland and his men. In fact, there was one incident that happened during their training that reveals how the will to fight was ultimately forged on the anvil of prejudice ..."

• • •

There they were, together in a military training camp sprawled on a cricket field in the middle of Truro, Nova Scotia, preparing to join a war many, both Black and white, felt they had no business being in. From Saint John and Sacramento, from Alberta and Africville, from farming villages, college classrooms, and urban ghettoes, some were barbers, others railway porters, preachers, or fishermen. They came because they believed, somehow, that wearing the uniform might change something, that loyalty might finally be rewarded with dignity.

Private Clemens McNeil leaned on his shovel, sweat streaking down his face, his broad hands blistered from the morning's labour.

"Never thought soldierin' would mean diggin' holes all day," he muttered, half to himself.

Clemens had travelled all the way to Truro from Shreveport, Louisiana, in the hope of joining the battalion. Many from the States, in fact, had made the sojourn, especially after facing significant racial discrimination and rejection from the U.S. military. Clergy and editors of Black newspapers urged African Americans to come forward and join the No. 2 Construction Battalion, which they portrayed as a righteous crusade in the fight for equality across the land. As the response grew, a training depot at Windsor, Ontario, was quickly established, providing access to a large population of African American men making their way across the Detroit River.

Fred Dixon drove his shovel into the dirt beside him. "Better holes here than graves over there," he replied, spitting in the grass. "Though mark my words, they'll have us doin' that soon enough."

George William, the battalion's trusted bandmaster, stood just a few feet away with his own shovel in hand. Lieutenant Colonel Sutherland had recently promoted him to sergeant, a position he took quite seriously among the men.

"Now boys," George William chided, "if we keep talking, we'll be here until night. And listenin' to you is not worth missin' dinner for."

Clemens smirked as he pushed his spade back into the dirt. Around them, the camp hummed with activity. Men drilled with old rifles under the barked orders of white officers. Others mended torn boots or washed their uniforms in buckets by the barracks. On the far end of the cricket field, a group of recruits enjoyed the reprieve of a baseball game, the crack of the bat echoing like a gunshot before laughter chased it. Music drifted from the mess tent — harmonicas, fiddles, and even a battered trumpet someone had brought from home.

At last, evening came, and the camp belonged to song. Hymns, work songs, and blues tangled together, a quilt of sound that floated up into the Truro sky. Voices carried past the railway lines, across the fields, and into the town itself — though not always welcomed there. Sometimes the townsfolk muttered about "noise." But for the soldiers, music was the joyful protest of hope.

One Saturday, word spread that a moving picture was playing in town. For weeks the men had been restless, itching for distraction, and when a handful asked for leave, the officers, mindful of the need to keep up morale, reluctantly agreed.

Clemens had never been to a theatre. "Imagine that," he said to Fred as they buttoned their coats, not hiding his excitement, "pictures movin' across a wall, big as life!"

"Hope it's worth the nickel," Fred said. "Could be nothin' but some fella scratchin' his bum for an hour."

The men laughed. They headed out with the group, their boots crunching on the gravel road as they marched into Truro. The town was small but proud, with red-brick storefronts and gas lamps lining the streets. Women bustled out of the baker's shop, the smell of fresh bread hanging in the air. Horses clopped along the road, wagons creaking under loads of timber.

The theatre was a tall white building with a glowing marquee. When the recruits reached the front doors, the usher — a thin man with a pressed cap — blocked their path.

"Coloreds don't sit down here," he said flatly. He jabbed a thumb toward a narrow staircase at the side. "Balcony only."

Fred stiffened. "We're soldiers," he snapped. "In uniform. Bound for France same as any other man."

"And here in Truro we have our own rules," the usher replied, eyes cold. "Soldier or not, don't make any difference."

The men bristled. Clemens closed in next to Fred. Behind him, another from the group muttered, "We'll bleed for this country but can't sit in your seats?!"

Voices rose. Townsfolk, sensing trouble, stopped to watch. Some whispered, others folded their arms, their faces a mixture of curiosity and disdain.

A local man stepped forward, glaring. "Best you boys take the balcony," he sneered. "Or take yourselves back where you came from."

Clemens stepped forward, his fists clenched. Fred gripped his comrade's arm. Tension thickened the air as the movement of a fight caught the crowd's attention. Angry words volleyed back and forth, sharp as bayonets.

An officer from camp appeared, running down the street. "That's enough!" he barked. His gaze swept over the recruits. "Back to barracks, all of you! Now!"

The men stood still as stone. "That's enough!" bellowed the officer. "I've given you orders!"

The group reluctantly retreated. They marched back, boots thudding against the gravel. That night, the barracks was a simmering cauldron of anger.

"Fightin' a war we ain't even wanted in," one man spat, pacing the floorboards. "And treated like dogs at home."

George had been sitting on the edge of his bunk, listening to the men recount what had happened. His head was half buried in his hands, but they could not hide his dejection. "For God's sake," he muttered, "we don't even get respect with a uniform on. What's the point of being here?"

Clemens pulled out a harmonica, running a thumb across its dented surface. "Same thing I'm thinking," he said to the room. "Can't watch a picture show, but they'll ship us off to France to break our backs in the mud. Tell me how that makes sense."

At that moment, George William stepped away from the post he was leaning against. "It don't," he responded. "But maybe — just maybe — someday our sons won't see the same. Maybe if we bear it now, they'll stand a little taller later. Somebody's gotta be first through the fire. Fellas, it's us who gotta see this through to the end — whatever the end may be."

The men fell quiet. Even the barracks stove seemed to submit its crackling to the reverent silence. Outside, the cricket field lay silver under the moon, the town's lights flickering faintly in the distance. A train whistle cut through the night, long and mournful.

The weeks dragged on, and the heaviness of training became harder to bear. Reveille at dawn. Drills until blisters bled. Endless hauling of timber, sharpening of nails, polishing of boots. Yet, despite the burdens, the spirit of the men grew in unexpected places. Their baseball games became the talk of camp, fierce matches where bats cracked and gloves snapped, and in these fleeting moments the men forgot the world around them. Even the officers came to watch and were compelled to cheer them on.

And, as always, music carried them. On Sunday evenings, voices rose in harmony — deep baritones and sharp tenors weaving hymns together. They sang of deliverance, of rivers wide and skies open. They sang for themselves, and for the generations yet to come. By lantern light, they would spin tales of home — of women they danced with until morning, of fishing trips that turned into feasts, of mothers who could feed a family on nothing but salt pork and hope. The younger recruits listened wide-eyed, clinging to those stories like lifelines to a better future.

Then, as the first snow melted in the early spring, the order came. The battalion would soon ship out. France. The word began to echo on the lips of the soldiers, repeated in hushes between every conversation. Some men wrote letters hurriedly, their pens scratching across thin paper. Others played cards until dawn, as if to delay the inevitable.

On their final night in Truro, Clemens walked to the edge of the cricket field. Wet snow lay over the grass, the air still carrying the cold chill of a retreating winter. He looked toward the glow of town, where the theatre stood with the memory of humiliation on its steps. He lifted his harmonica and played. A slow, mournful tune rose into the night. Others gathered around him, listening. The melody held their sorrow, their anger, their pride. It carried their spirit like a prayer.

When the last note faded, Clemens whispered, "Someday, they'll remember us."

And in the hush that followed, every man hoped he was right.

• • •

As my dad leans back in his chair, I am still weighing the burden of prejudice these men had to carry onto the battlefield.

I remark out loud, "I can see why they spoke so little about their time as soldiers."

My dad looks at me. "I'm afraid, son, it only begins to explain their silence about the war. What happened while they were over there … one can imagine hell, but to live through it, well that's another thing entirely."

I turn to the faces of the men staring back at me from the photo of the battalion's marching band. What memories am I looking into, hidden behind a hundred years of silence?

My question is interrupted by my father's voice. "Son, would you help me get up? I need to go for a walk."

I lead Dad down the pathway toward his back alley, where he enjoys strolling in the quiet lane, now covered by a canopy of damp autumn elms. As he carefully moves on, I lean against a tree and look up into the bright yellow leaves that stand out against the grey sky. What exactly did my grandfather go through on the battlefields of France over a century ago? I decide it's the next question my father and I must answer.

7

The Silent War

The most potent weapon in the hands of the oppressor is the mind of the oppressed.

—STEPHEN BIKO, *I Write What I Like*

There is a small book called *The Black Battalion 1916–1920: Canada's Best Kept Military Secret*. It's a collection of stories and artifacts from surviving veterans written by Calvin Ruck, a man who deserves his own chapter in the history of Canada. Over his lifetime, Calvin Ruck received several honours and awards for his work in racial justice, including the Order of Canada, as well as honorary degrees from Dalhousie University and the University of

King's College. In 1998, Ruck became only the third Black Canadian ever to be appointed to the Senate. Born to immigrant parents from Barbados, Calvin started from humble roots in small town rural Nova Scotia. As for so many people of colour growing up in this country, his road to success was marked by the obstacles of prejudice. For instance, in 1954, Ruck and his wife bought a small plot of land in a white suburb of Halifax. Right away, a petition was signed by local residents to bar them from building a home there. Though the town could not find legal grounds to remove them from their neighbourhood, Ruck was deeply demoralized. Eventually, it became the fire that motivated him to champion the fight against discrimination in this country.

Not long after that experience, Calvin found work on the railway. He started to notice a few of the older Black porters wearing a strange small pin on their suit coats. When he inquired about these pins, he was told they were worn by the veterans who served in what they called "the Black Battalion." As he traversed the thousands of kilometres across the country, huddled in the back of rail cars during many long nights, Calvin listened intently to the incredible ordeals they faced during the First World War. He became determined to "pay a lasting tribute" to the men who not only fought on the front lines of the war, but also battled the injustice of racism back home. In the introduction of his book, Ruck writes:

> Many Canadians of all races have no idea that Blacks served, fought, bled and died on European battlefields, all in the name of freedom. The fact that approximately six hundred Black soldiers served in a segregated non-combatant labour battalion during World War One has been one of the best kept secrets in Canadian military history.

Ironically, the book is not widely known. I was able to acquire a copy through my involvement in the national advisory committee for the upcoming national apology. For so many descendants, the movement for a national apology has been a profound learning experience, for it has brought to light many new stories and information about the men who fought in the war. In the middle pages of his book, Calvin Ruck inserted the same photo of the No. 2 Construction Battalion marching band that my father had in his living room. Sitting cross-legged on the ground, in the middle of the small group of men, is my grandfather, his uniform hat tilted over his brow, proudly holding his cornet. Around him, his band members stare into the

Cap badge worn by soldiers of the No. 2 Construction Battalion.

camera, all posed equally proudly. In their own way, they represented the hopes and dreams, struggles and heartaches of Black communities across this country, who believed they had a rightful place in the story of this nation.

On March 28, 1917, these soldiers, along with the other members of the No. 2 Construction Battalion, embarked from Pier 2 at Halifax and set off for war. For three of the men, that was the last voyage they ever sailed, for they died on the ship from the flu that overtook the crew. Death had come upon the battalion before they even reached the shores of France. As for the rest, after two weeks of sailing through submarine-infested waters, they were sent directly to the front lines of the war on the eastern border of France.

The most reliable firsthand account of what happened during the war comes from the diary of Captain Andrew White, a Black Baptist minister who served as chaplain to the battalion and was its only Black officer. White's great-nephew, Anthony Sherwood, is a talented actor and film producer, and some years ago he directed a docudrama based on his great-uncle's diary entitled *Honour Before Glory*. In the film, we witness the character of Captain White recount the gruelling work of Black soldiers in the battalion, how they would scramble ahead to buttress the trenches and secure the ladders for the white soldiers to climb up into the fray of the battlefields, and then quickly lash the poles that would carry the wounded white soldiers back to the camps. But when a Black soldier fell, they had to be carried by their own, then placed in segregated tents to wait for treatment.

It was such a blatant demonstration of prejudice that Captain White made a point of recording the numerous instances when Black soldiers were left unattended. In the end, it was often not in battle where these Black soldiers died, but in the field hospitals where infections were left untreated. Given all that we know about the battalion, there are very few personal testimonies from the soldiers themselves beyond Captain White's diary. It's like the collective memories of the battalion members were suppressed the moment their feet touched the soil back home.

Of course, I'm particularly interested to know more about my own grandfather's experience overseas. After lunch, I help Dad return to his lounge chair in the living room.

"So, Dad, I need to ask you a question. You have never spoken about Papa's experience during the war, whether it be memories or stories, or even how he felt about being there after it was all over."

Dad sighs, then nods slowly. "It's because your papa never spoke of it." He leans over to his magazine holder. "Will you pull out that brown envelope there? It came from your cousin Eunice the other day."

I bring it onto my lap and pull out a stack of what looks like military files. I begin to leaf through the pages as my dad leans back, patiently waiting. Halfway through the third page, I stop.

"Dad … I didn't know. His war record — it was so troubled."

"Neither did I. It explains his silence, I guess. But the truth has a way of finding the light, even when we'd rather not see it."

"I don't get it," I say, shaking my head. "Why would he act that way? There's hardly any explanation here — just scribbled notes from officers. It leaves more questions than answers."

"Many of the men in No. 2 Battalion struggled," Dad says quietly. "After all, they faced racism every single day."

"So, Papa wasn't the only one?"

"No," Dad explains. "It's been said that almost a third of the men in No. 2 were punished for so-called serious offences. Some even faced courts-martial. But you have to understand — segregation weighs down the spirit of any man. They were isolated, treated unfairly, pushed to the margins. Discipline was bound to crumble."

I stare at the folder again. "Makes sense. So, Papa's behaviour wasn't just about him. It was about the system."

"Yes," Dad firmly states. "Your papa wasn't a bad man — he was a man trapped in a bad situation. Men can only bend so much. At some point, even the good ones break."

That afternoon, over several hours, piece by piece, a profile of a conflicted soldier was laid before me. His military record read like a litany of one misconduct after another. It was heartbreaking, really, to read what my grandfather had done during the war. My father was right, though: Many Black soldiers had enlisted believing they would be given the chance to fight. Frustration at this second-class treatment, coupled with crowded living conditions, as well as alcohol, boredom, and poor leadership, would have all been factors in creating harmful and disruptive behaviour. Denied the chance to prove themselves on equal terms, many soldiers of the battalion came to feel betrayed, and their anger turned inward, against officers and even against their own comrades.

Through this lens, I felt like I could talk about the impact the war had on my grandfather without diminishing his dignity. As I continued to sift through the pages, the real story of what happened to him during the war started to emerge. At this point, it is the most difficult moment of his life to share, but I know it's important to finally bring closure to a chapter that had, until now, seemed lost to the grave.

• • •

Seymour crept into the barracks and leaned close to George, his voice barely above a whisper. "Hey — you hear what happened?"

George looked up, wary. "What now?"

"Private Jackson," Seymour said, uneasy. "Him and two fellas went drinking down Censeau Road. Came back loud … fight broke out. Cane swinging, fists flying. Jackson went down hard. They carried him off into a field."

"A field?" George frowned. "Why not the infirmary?"

Seymour shrugged. "Dunno. But he ain't come back. Not a sign of him for two days."

George shot up from his bunk, his shoulders stiff. "You saying he's still out there?"

"That's the word."

Silence hung between them. George paced, jaw tight. "So that's it? A man don't return, and nobody moves a muscle?"

"Careful, George," Seymour urged. "Could just be talk —"

"Talk or not, it stinks," George cut in. "If it were one of *them*, they'd have a whole search party out. But us? Just another Black body gone missing."

Seymour pressed his friend. "Let's wait and see. Maybe Captain Livingston —"

"Livingston?" George snapped. "He won't lift a finger." He grabbed his coat.

"Where you going?" Seymour asked nervously.

"To find him myself. If Jackson's lying in some ditch, someone ought to bring him home."

Before George reached the door, Seymour stepped in front of him. "Don't, George. We got orders — they might throw you in the stockade if you go without leave."

George froze, fists clenched, his body trembling with anger. His voice dropped low. "Orders. Always orders. Meanwhile, a man's life don't count for nothin'."

"Easy, brother," Seymour whispered. "We'll watch. We'll wait. But don't let this eat you alive."

George stared into the shadows, then shoved past and disappeared. Seymour sank back onto his cot, head heavy in his hands.

Hours later, George stumbled into the barracks, rubbing his sore arm. Seymour jerked awake, "George? What the hell happened?"

"I took a horse to go find Jackson, is what happened," George muttered. "Livingston caught up with me in the motor car and had me dragged back. Officers damn near pulled my arm off."

"George," Seymour warned, "you're gonna get in worse trouble if you don't let things go —"

"Let what go, Seymour?" George exploded. "One of our men's out there, and they don't care if he lives or dies. Our lives don't matter, Seymour." He turned away, his voice lower now. "I'm gonna clean the barn. Can't stand doin' nothin'."

When Private Michael Jackson was finally found, battered and near death in a field near the military camp, George was called to testify at the inquiry. He told them what he knew about the fight between the soldiers, about his own search for his comrade and the dismissal from the officer, and about the silence afterward. In the day following George's testimony, Jackson was pronounced dead from his head injuries. A couple more soldiers were called to testify. Word soon got around, though, that officers had moved on from the investigation of Jackson's death for lack of credible witnesses. A few days later he was buried in a communal cemetery close to the French village of Champagnole.

A couple of weeks passed. One afternoon, through a chill blanket of fog, Seymour approached the stockades. Inside, the heavy, damp air felt oppressive. In the corner cell, a single bench was pushed against the wall. George was hunched over it, his face buried in his arms. Seymour appeared at the bars.

"George … George, can you hear me?" Seymour's voice was awkward, almost pleading. "I heard you got arrested and came right away." Silence met him. He pressed on. "George, I wish you'd talk to me. The officer said you could've killed him, the way you swung that razor blade. Being out all night drinking was bad enough — but to pick a fight with an officer? What were you thinking?"

George lifted his head, eyes dark. "How you get outta hell, Seymour. That's what I was thinkin' — how do I get outta hell?"

"Well … it ain't by the bottle," Seymour said gently. "Gettin' drunk every day ain't gonna help you get out any sooner —"

George snapped up, bitter. "And what of it? You think they care if I rot here? They never cared … just ask Jackson when he lay dying in that field."

"That night … it ain't on you," Seymour insisted, leaning closer. "You did what you could."

"And he still died," George shot back, voice hollow. "Left in the dark like he was nothin'. That's what we are here — nothing."

"Don't say that," pleaded Seymour.

George's voice was cold as stone. "Our lives don't matter, Seymour."

"No," Seymour said firmly. "Not in here they don't. Look at you, George — you're a mess. C'mon, we can still make the best of what we have. There's still a chance to make a difference, to make this all worth somethin'." His voice softened, almost pleading. "Remember how we said we'd come here and show them we could fight?"

George's eyes flashed. "With what, Seymour? Pickaxes and shovels? 'Cause that's what they gave us. Did you notice they dumped us in a forest — to cut trees in the cold rain? Threw us in trenches — to dig. While bombs burst the ground open, we're scrambling to build bridges." His voice cracked. "Yeah, Seymour, we sure showin' 'em how we can fight."

"Look around, Seymour. Who we fightin'? With all the rage we got in our bones we could take on the Fritz just ourselves — but instead we left here to turn our hate on each other. Ask any of these men what we gained by being here, if they feel we made any difference at all. All I see is what we lost. Our pride is gone — lost in those damn forests, Seymour, buried in those trenches …"

Seymour lowered his head, silence pressing between them.

George leaned back, voice bereft of life. "No — I'm fine in here. Thank you very much."

Seymour turned away, his steps heavy. Back in the barracks, he sat on his cot, staring into the dark.

In the months that passed, far from George retrieving any purpose for being in the war, his heart only hardened. A few weeks after he was released, he was reprimanded again for causing a drunken disturbance in the soldiers' camp during the early afternoon. The officers stripped George of his regular duties and subjected him to what was mercilessly called the "crucifixion," a form of punishment where he was roped to a wheel for two hours a day. Apparently, it did little to purge his anger. Showing little reform, George was relegated to mess hall and latrine duties until the war ended.

On January 17, 1919, after being tasked with the thankless job of cleaning up the remnants of the war and battle camps, George was finally sent home. By then, the parades and fanfare had all but come to an end. He returned to Canadian soil with only silent memories and a broken spirit.

Indeed, when the men of the No. 2 Construction Battalion finally came home in the winter of 1919, the welcome was nothing like they had pictured. After months overseas, they stepped off the ships *Olympic* and *Empress of Britain* onto the Halifax docks. The air was sharp with cold, but there were no bands playing, no flags waving, no crowds cheering their return. Instead, each man was handed a rail travel pass and seventy dollars — the price of his service. One by one, they disappeared from history.

In fact, the battalion's efforts were erased almost as soon as they ended. When the Canadian Forestry Corps published a record of their service later that year, it made no mention of the Black construction battalion at all. To anyone reading, it was as if they had never existed. Even the gravestones of men who had died overseas left out the truth of who they were and what unit they had served.

Back in their hometowns, the men quickly realized that nothing had changed. The same prejudice and discrimination they had known before the war still followed them. For George and his friends, the armistice had not ended their fight. They pushed their service overseas aside, for their real battle — the struggle to live with dignity in a world that refused to see them — was far from over.

• • •

I look over to see my dad staring into the photo.

"During the five years I served in the air force," he says softly, "I was never sent overseas to fight. Every day, if you think about it, soldiers are training with the clear thought of dying. Your grandfather had to face two wars, the one on the field and the one in his soul. There's no question war brings out the best — and worst — in us. I can see now how both wars did that to your papa."

As I listen intently to my father, I sense there is more to my grandfather's story I have yet to learn. But right now, I feel I need to celebrate the redemptive light cast over this chapter of my grandfather's life. He showed a fierce determination to fight for the dignity of his comrade. He was not prepared to let racism diminish the man's worth. My grandfather was not willing to feel helpless in the moment, nor let status determine his power to do what he felt was right. And yet, I understand how the disappointment of not being able to help his comrade would turn into bitterness. He's not alone: Countless men and women have lost hope in the face of lifelong oppression. It just breaks my heart to think that my grandfather became overwhelmed by the darkness that in that moment, however fleeting, he felt his own light could overcome.

8

Life as a Footnote

It is easier to build strong children than to repair broken men.

—FREDERICK DOUGLASS, American abolitionist and author

The next morning, my father and I are quietly sitting in the front room of his small bungalow as a storm settles over the city. For a while I'm content drinking my coffee, watching the rain roll down the windows, and hearing the claps of thunder echo across the prairies. It's also the time of day when Dad is eager to listen to one of the many podcasts that a fellow retired pastor is fond of sending him. It's always an ordeal getting the app on his iPad set up properly, but once it starts, he's quite happy closing his eyes and taking in the narration.

I'm just finishing my second cup when Dad slips the headset off and looks around.

"Ah, son, could you get me another cup of coffee?"

After returning with his mug, I decide the time has come to ask a question that is weighing heavily on my mind. Over these last few days, as I listened to my father share all the stories about his own father, from all his childhood adventures to his tribulations during the war, I learned so much about how life shaped Papa into the man he became. But how did my grandfather shape my father into the man *he* became? To what extent did my dad as a boy feel the effect of his father's trauma from the war? Did he remove barriers of racism, or chart a path to greater purpose that my father would one day follow? How did he influence my father? And in turn, how did that influence the kind of man *I* had become? This seems the best chance I have to find these answers.

"Dad, you've mentioned a few times that life was not always easy growing up with Papa. How so?"

I can see by the expression on my father's face that he is struggling to find the right place to begin. No doubt, I'm asking my father to recall moments in his life that after all these years he had chosen not to speak of for a reason. But in our recent time together, he has hinted there is something about his father he needs to reconcile, a lingering wound that finally needs healing.

When my father does begin, it's at a place I don't expect.

"You know," he muses, "I don't think I've said much about your nana. I suppose you could write a whole book on her. Your nana, Muriel, the eldest of two daughters, had a mother from Indiantown who was as fiery and fierce as they come. Mary Hogan was her name."

"Hogan," I interrupt, "I'm sure you once said your mother's maiden name was Goldsmith — tell me more about her father."

"Ah, Stanley Goldsmith," my father beams, "the most unlikely fellow for your great-grandmother to fall in love with! Stanley had spent most of his childhood on a ship full of delinquent boys off the coast of Australia. Apparently, around the end of the nineteenth century, the government from 'down under' had devised this floating reformatory to address the epidemic of homeless boys wandering about the streets. The idea was to teach them how to contribute to society or, if that failed, enlist them in the navy. Stanley's fate was the latter."

This whole backdrop to my great-grandfather is like opening another wild chapter to history from across the world. "So how did they meet?" I ask.

"Apparently, Stanley didn't much take to being a sailor. While on leave at the port of Saint John, he disappeared. And it seems the Australian authorities were quite happy abandoning their wayward cadet to the hinterland of Canada, for they sailed off without him! Well, Stanley didn't waste time getting himself acquainted to this strange new world. It turns out he was quite the charmer, especially with the young ladies. He even somehow managed to sweep your great-grandmother off her feet — which is impressive given how miserable a person she was."

"A most unusual tale of romance indeed," I quip.

"Well, it didn't last long. They had two girls, Muriel, your grandmother, and Beatrice, your great-aunt — otherwise known as Bea. Eventually, though, dealing with your great-grandmother became too much for Stanley. One day he simply up and left her, leaving Mary to raise the two girls on her own. Last I heard, Stanley had joined an acting troupe in Toronto and got married to a girl half his age. But anything about Stanley Goldsmith after he left your great-grandmother would amount to rumour, really."

"Wow," I comment, "I guess that explains why few in the family ever spoke about him."

"Given your great-grandmother's disposition," my dad explains, "it's little surprise she said nothing about Muriel's father once he walked out the door. Shortly after Stanley disappeared, Mary managed to get another husband. His name was Josiah Holmes. She changed her name to Mary Holmes, had five more children, and life carried on. As the years passed, though, everyone in Indiantown had a pretty good idea Josiah was not the real father of Muriel and Bea. Both girls were fairly light skinned with long, narrow facial features and bore little resemblance to Josiah. Most were convinced that their real father was probably a man from among the First Nation folk who still lived around Indiantown. Right through my childhood, we would talk in hushed tones about our mother and aunt being 'part squaw' — that, I must confess, is how we spoke back then."

And then, with a wide grin, my father leans forward and whispers, "It turns out, Muriel knew something about her father that I would discover much later. Stanley Goldsmith, your grandmother's real father, was actually *Jewish*!"

Having revealed this family secret, my father sits back and takes a deep sip of his coffee as I try to get my head around this bewildering tale of my great-grandfather. In some ways, it kind of answered a few puzzling pieces in our family lore that never seemed to add up. In promoting cultural competency, one of my tasks as a race equity educator is to encourage teachers to explore the oral tradition within students' home cultures as a vital source of knowledge about one's rightful place in history. I often share a remarkable story I heard a few years ago while working with a teacher in a small francophone school on the north side of downtown. Their son, Josiah, was Haitian-born and raised within their Indigenous and white family in Calgary. He had signed up to play in a youth Indigenous basketball tournament and was denied entry. This mother shared how it broke their adopted son's heart. Furthermore, she explained, it broke the sacred meaning among her husband's Heiltsuk Nation of what it means to be adopted.

In hearing the plight of this young man, Yasmine Mathurin, a young Haitian-born filmmaker living in Calgary, made the documentary *One of Ours*, which follows the family's odyssey to reclaim their son's right to play basketball in a tournament for Indigenous youth. In the film, Josiah's father argues that the organizers of this province-wide tournament had reduced identity to "blood quantum," a colonial construct that was used to eliminate his people over generations. In contrast, the Heiltsuk traditional law of adoption is a sacred bond, used to strengthen relations within and among other nations. Adoption is essentially the ceremony to honour those whom they are committed to love, regardless of their ethnic or cultural origins. Above all, argues the father, to practise the custom is a means to practise sovereignty over who they decide is part of their nation and how they define their identity.

Mathurin spent almost five years on the project. As she told the CBC, witnessing the Heiltsuk way of belonging unfold as they collectively fought for their sovereign right to choose who is part of their nation reminded the filmmaker of her own journey as a Haitian immigrant and her elusive identity as a Canadian.* During production, racial conflict erupted in the wake of the George Floyd murder, and she had to wrestle with the same questions about identity that the film's subjects were facing.

Each of us finds ourselves navigating at least one element of social identity. Something as innocuous as skin colour has always created a complicated narrative in my life. I am a light-skinned person of mixed racial heritage who usually passes as white in most social settings, at least in Canada. However, my first consciousness of identity was formed in Detroit where, by virtue of American laws, I was politically and socially categorized as Black because of my father. Regardless of the colour of my skin, the law stated that by virtue of possessing one-eighth Black heritage (in some states the proportion was as little as one-sixteenth), being *Black* was my official racial status. In this complicated world, we end up arriving at very different places in relation to these constructed identities.

Let's look at it another way. What does it mean for a person of colour who was adopted into a comfortable middle-class white home in the suburbs and grew up completely disconnected from the oppressive conditions of a racialized

---

* CBC Docs, "Award-Winning Filmmaker Shares Struggles of a Young Haitian Adopted into an Indigenous Family in Canada," January 17, 2022, cbc.ca/documentaries/award-winning-filmmaker-shares-struggles-of-a-young-haitian-adopted-into-an-indigenous-family-in-canada-1.6317733.

community on the margins of society? Outside of the occasional racist remarks, would that person have the same level of *consciousness* about the injustices that have plagued people of colour over generations? And would they have a full appreciation of the cultural reality that has shaped how that community sees the world from the margins? (To illustrate my point, have a quick look at '90s television show *The Fresh Prince of Bel-Air*.)

Conversely, what if a person is adopted into a racialized community, such as an Indigenous First Nation, and shares similar enough skin complexion to naturally experience how others within this community are treated by those *outside* the community? Basically, my point is that identity is far more complex than the colour of skin, or the blood of ancestry. Our sense of identity is also legitimated by *our proximity to the culture in which our consciousness has been shaped.*

My contemplation is interrupted by my father. He is stretching over the arm of his chair, fumbling to make room for his mug on the table beside him. He finally finds a spot, then leans back again. "Now, where was I?"

"You were talking about your mother's father, Stanley, but it began with me asking about your relationship with your own father ..."

"Ah, yes, I remember where I was going with this. You see, once I understood who my mother's real father was, it all made sense why she showed such loyalty to the Jewish homes she worked for as a cleaner. In fact, your nana remained faithful to one particular Jewish family until the end of her working days. There was something about that relationship that mattered deeply to her. I think that longing to connect to her father's side was a result of being treated so horribly by her mother. Her younger sister, Bea, was a precocious child, to put it mildly. She was always getting into places and situations that she really had no business being in. And each time, your nana, Muriel, did her best to bail her younger sister out of trouble.

"And by sticking her neck out for her little sister, it meant taking the heat from their mother. And let me remind you, your great-grandmother had a hot temper! But, despite the abuse she endured at the hands of her own mother, Muriel never stopped loving her little sister — and neither did she stop longing for a family of her own. She was, from the beginning, a kind-hearted woman, your nana, whose commitment to her family roots stayed strong till the very end."

My dad looks wistfully into the distance. I'm still not sure why he's spending so much time reminiscing about his mother, but as the corners of his eyes begin to glisten, it's clear he cherishes these memories of her.

A long moment passes before my dad clears his eyes and turns to me. "Son, as I tell you what happened between my father and I, try to see him through the eyes of my mother who, like a saint, loved the man to the very end."

I reverently nod in agreement.

"Good," my father replies, "then let me tell you what I remember about my father growing up."

• • •

After the war, your papa returned to live with his aunt Cassie on Spar Cove Road. Muriel was living with her mother and siblings just a few houses up the road. She was now a young woman and eager to start a family. George, however, was still a restless soul. He was in no way ready to settle down. He tried his hand at a few jobs in town, even as a fireman, but nothing came of it. Finally, after several frustrating months back from the war, in early January of 1920, he headed to sea again on board the ship *Maskinonge.* Only a few months later, though, he landed back on shore in Louisbourg, Nova Scotia. It became his last voyage on the sea. With a little less than eighty dollars in his pocket, George headed back to his life on Spar Cove Road. It seemed he finally had enough of life on his own, for soon after he returned, George and Muriel got married. Their first home together was an apartment along Sheriff Street, in the north end of the city, where a small Black community dwelt. They didn't last long there. The city had let the neighbourhood become derelict, and shortly after they had moved in the city began demolishing the houses.

So, they moved to another small Black community along Union Alley — and this was truly an alley. It was nothing more than six dilapidated row houses built along a dead-end laneway behind the Old Opera House off Union Street in downtown Saint John. On each floor of these row houses lived a different family. Now, if you add up how many kids were in each house, and multiply that by the number of houses, well you get an idea of how that alley was a town all by itself! Hidden in the heart of the city was a whole community of Black folk who cooked for each other, worked with each other, and brought children into the world together. Nana White, as we called her, lived as a widow with her three boys on the first floor of our house. Hermie, her oldest, eventually married Phyllis, my second oldest sister. And then Carl, her second oldest, ended up marrying Jean, my third oldest sister. Before long we hardly knew — or cared — which floor of the house any of their children belonged to! Such was life on Union Alley.

Mr. Hopkins was the landlord of the houses in this alley. He was an older white gentleman, and thankfully quite generous at heart. That's my impression at least, because in all my time growing up there, I can't say if we ever paid rent. I vividly remember Mr. Hopkins standing on the steps chatting with my mother on the first day of every month, kindly exchanging words. But in all these instances, only a few times do I recall seeing my mother hand him money. I suspect Mr. Hopkins took one look at the countless mouths she was trying to feed, and out of a great deal of pity offered a quiet word of forgiveness of what she owed and walked away.

As we got older, none of us ended up spending much time in the house. There was no use. Mama never expected us to show up at a certain time for dinner, or bed for that matter. Now, I knew from other kids at school they had rules, but in our house we just came and left as we needed. We had one sink in our house, with one faucet of cold water. In the winter, when the pipes froze, that was the other time we saw Mr. Hopkins. He and Mama would furiously get at clearing those pipes, one wrapping towels soaked in boiled water along the line while the other poured water from the stove down the drain.

The only real routine I remember as a boy was taking turns bringing your papa his dinner, especially as the years wore on. The ladies in the alley always had a cup of tea in the afternoon. And then the baking and cooking would happen. And when the food was cooled, the child closest to the house would be the one called in to bring the first plate to Papa. As he grew older, and his drinking became more frequent, Papa became more aggressive and short-tempered, which made the task of delivering his food an anxious one for me. Your papa had always seemed more comfortable with his oldest boys. I would watch him grab the shoulders of my older brothers, Leonard, Hilton and Franky, and listen as he approvingly exclaimed to each one of them, "You're my boy!" As for me, I barely even got a look from him. For various reasons, I suppose, he showed little affection toward me. As a child I couldn't make him proud no matter what I did. I liked going to church — he disdained religion. I liked school and books — he thought it was a waste of time and figured boys should work as soon as they were strong enough. As I got older, I became less accepting of my father, less seeking of his approval.

Over time, Papa no longer hid his disdain for me, to the point that Mama wouldn't let us be left alone in the same room. Especially when I became a teenager, I think she became real afraid of a confrontation between us. In fact, looking back I realize how much she altered her day so she could be home to protect me. To his credit, in those days I don't think Papa ever missed a day of work. He would come home exhausted from laying bricks or other construction jobs. Despite being tired, though, he never failed to read the newspaper after dinner. Front to back he would pore over it, including advertisements for things he would not even conceive of buying. He would read the gossip column and the comic section, until finally he exhausted every page. *What for?* I would say rather cynically to myself. *It takes him all night just to finish the damn thing.* Looking back, maybe Papa was trying to keep up with what the other men were discussing on the construction site, like the current news, or forecasts about the coming weather, or what wives are shopping for these days. Perhaps it was a vain attempt at maintaining his sense of place among men. But as I said, it made little sense to me back then.

On the weekend, Papa would bring home his pay and give it to your nana. She would then give him enough money for his case of beer, which he would promptly go purchase and carry back to his room. For most of the weekend he would sit alone in there and drink. On occasion, one of his friends would come by, and together they would disappear down to the legion. But on Sunday, he basically drank by himself while Mama headed off to church with most of us kids in tow. As for me, every Saturday morning I would walk to the Anglican mission church down the hill to help Father Mark with the 7:30 a.m. Mass. I'm not sure why I enjoyed going to church; none of my siblings went. But Father Mark was one of those figures in my life who genuinely expressed appreciation for me, and that meant a lot at the time. And I did believe in God — your nana instilled that faith in me, for she was a devout Christian woman. She also had a strong sense of what was right — and wrong — in the world. She saw the hypocrisy of the Church of England putting up separate buildings down the hill for Black folk to have their services. She didn't object to me attending on Saturday mornings, but Mama made it clear that she "wouldn't give a penny to them Anglicans." She felt much more comfortable in the local Baptist congregation that was at least led by a pastor from our own Black community.

One Saturday morning, just before heading off to Mass, I discovered my father's cornet in the broom closet. When I walked into the kitchen with it, your nana insisted I put it back and leave it alone. She knew I wanted to play music, and it seemed a waste for it just to be sitting there. I should have listened to her. Instead, a few weeks later I decided not to go to the local gym after Mass and came home early. The house was unusually silent. For a moment I idly stood in the middle of the living room, until temptation led me to the closet where my father's cornet lay in the corner. I pulled it out, then sat cross-legged on the thin carpet of the apartment, the brass cornet heavy in my lap. I lifted it to my lips and was trying to coax out notes when the door banged open.

My father stood in the doorway, his eyes dark with a yet unspoken terror and fury, locked on the instrument.

"Get your hands off that!" he yelled, crossing the room in three strides.

I jerked back, clutching the cornet to my chest. My father reached in and tried to yank it away. The two of us struggled, our hands fumbling in a tense, wordless battle until at last my father tore it free. He set the cornet down hard on the bench, the metal ringing with finality.

"When are you gonna become a man?" His voice shook.

Without thinking, I said defiantly, "Oh, what — like you?"

For a second, silence pressed between us.

"You have no idea, none," my father spat, trembling now, "what I've gone through to become who I am!"

He jabbed a finger at the cornet. "You think playing that will bring you any good? You think it'll make life easier? Do something that'll make you strong in this world."

My eyes burned, but I didn't look away. "Oh, like what?"

My father faltered. His voice cracked, raw. "The things you do — they'll amount to nothing. Religion, books, *music* — they'll get you nowhere in this life …"

"How do I know," I pleaded, "if I don't even get the chance to try?"

Something shifted in my father's face. He turned away, shoulders heaving as though the words had cut deeply. Then he swung back, his face now showing his own defiance.

"Then go! Try! See what you make of yourself. See what this world makes of you. I wish you would." His chest rose and fell, his fists clenched at his sides. "Then maybe you'd understand what it made of me."

9

A Father's Confession

Without memory, there is no healing, without forgiveness, there is no future.

—**ARCHBISHOP DESMOND TUTU,**
South African anti-apartheid
activist and peace campaigner

As my father recounts this moment, my eyes fall to the floor. At some level, my heart grieves for him for having to endure such painful disdain from his own father. At the same time, a lingering resentment surfaces over the disappointment I felt from him when I was growing up. I remember one time when I was fourteen years old and broke my collarbone playing hockey. It was days before I felt comfortable even doing normal things again, like sitting at a school desk and taking a bath. Meanwhile, our hockey team was struggling on the defensive line, and during a practice where I was watching from the boards, the coach hinted to my dad that he was anxious to have me back on the ice. I remember my father glancing over at me with a doubtful look.

In the week following, I tried to convince myself I would be fine, that the persistent pain would be nothing once I got on the ice. I told my dad I wanted to play in the next game. As the game started, I was filled with dread waiting on the bench for the coach to call me for my first shift. Sure enough, halfway through my shift an opponent drove a hard check into my left side. Instantly, a sharp pain shot from my shoulder to my neck. I recoiled and fell to the ice. I pushed myself up and started toward the bench, slapping my stick for somebody to jump on to replace me. As I slumped onto the bench, the coach came and stood over me, asking what was going on. It was hard for me to get my words out. Less than a minute later my father was leaning over the back of the bench, asking why I had left the game. I sat beneath these two men, shutting my eyes in an effort to hold in the pain, for I saw their frustration in me.

"Does it still hurt?" my father asked.

"No, I just thought it did," I muttered.

I sighed and opened my eyes, in time to see the coach look at my father with some consternation and disappear to the other end of the bench. My father stood there for a second longer and then turned away without even looking at me. I sat there, alone, for the rest of the game.

A week later, my mother told me that the coach had called while I was at school and suggested I play on a different league for the rest of the season, a recreation league that doesn't allow physical contact during games. I felt so demoralized. I was a good player, and I didn't know why they gave up on me so easily. My mom ended up driving me to a couple of games, and then I told her I didn't want to go anymore. My father never spoke to me about it.

And now, sitting across from him, listening to his own experience of confronting his father's disappointment in him, I'm not sure how to reconcile my memory with the one that he has carried for so long. I suppose it's enough for me to be mindful of how deeply we embody our trauma and pass it on without even realizing it. I decide it's better to press on in the hope of understanding more fully what happened between them.

"I can imagine, Dad, those words were enough to send you out the door."

"Pretty close to it." My father sighs and continues his story …

• • •

In the months that followed, my father and I barely spoke. I was getting close to graduating high school, and I had no idea what I was going to do once I finished, but I needed to get out. So I came home from school one day and told my mama I had to leave. I vowed not to return for at least a year, the time I decided it would take to figure out how to be my own man. I loved my mama, and I know she loved me, but I couldn't rely on her to protect me my whole life. I had just turned eighteen, and it was time I did something to prove I could stand on my own two feet in this world.

A couple of weeks before the end of school, I was home studying for my final papers. In those days, wrestling and boxing were popular, especially in our community. There was a boxing event at the forum that night, with a golden glove match on the card. Most people had gone early in order to get the best seats. The last one to get ready was my older sister Beatrice, who we called B.I. She was still in the bath. The rest of the three-storey house was pretty quiet. Nana White had just put the six grandkids to bed on the first floor. The Millers had left their two youngest girls on the second floor for the night, as they were going to the late-night church service at the Kingdom Hall. Their girls were Carol and Sylvia, probably nine and seven years old at the time. On their way out, Mrs. Miller called up for me to keep an ear out for them in case they needed anything, and off they went.

Of course, Papa was alone in his room. At this point in his life, he was just … existing. There was a time when he would go to the legion and visit with the boys. And he had other buddies who would sit out in the alley and shoot the breeze with him. But he stopped all that as time went on, to the point that he didn't talk to anybody or go anyplace unless Mama insisted he get out of the house. In contrast, Mama was finally making an effort to enjoy a bit of social life. That evening, she even decided to go to the boxing match, which surprised everyone. And thank God she did.

It must have been a little past eight o'clock. There I was, at my desk and lost in my books, when I heard shrieking coming from the floor beneath me. I realized right away it was Carol, the Millers' oldest girl. I rushed downstairs to see her standing in the hallway, smoke billowing out from the door behind her. I rushed over and pulled her away. I told her to run downstairs and tell Nana White to get the kids out of the house. As she took off down the stairs, I yelled for everyone to get out. Papa appeared at our doorway. Without pausing or saying a word, he stumbled past me and disappeared down the stairs. I looked back up to our apartment. No one else was coming, and with shame I realized that my father didn't have the capacity at the time to help. I fled up the stairs. As I yelled for Beatrice to get out of the house, I rushed into my parent's room and grabbed my little niece, Rosalind, who was staring at me wide-eyed from the back of the crib.

As I headed for the stairs, I again yelled behind me for B.I. to get out — there was no response.

By now there were screams and shouting from below. In a panic I stumbled down the stairs and out of the house. I remember thrusting my niece into somebody's arms. Turning quickly back toward the house, I saw that smoke now filled the front entrance. I only thought about my sister still up there, completely unaware that the house was burning. Truth be told, B.I. was more than just a sister to me, she was my best friend. More than any of my siblings, she and I really connected. She was the one I talked to the most, sharing things that I even couldn't tell Mama. Whatever it took, I was going to get my sister out of that house.

As I approached the steps, I took a deep breath and then plunged through the smoke toward the stairs. I just made it to the second-floor landing when I heard screaming from the apartment across the hallway. I froze. Little Sylvia was still in the house. I looked up the stairs. Our doorway at the top was hidden by smoke. Hearing the girl screaming again, I realized there was only one thing to do. I rushed to the door of my neighbour's apartment. I tried to enter, but I was immediately overcome with ashes and smoke searing across my face. I backed away. The screams, though, continued. I could barely make out Sylvia's small figure standing just inside the bedroom at the far end of the apartment, frozen in terror. I covered my face with my arms and stumbled across the smoke-filled room to where the girl was standing. As I reached down to grab her, I felt my lungs burning and the heat pulsing off the poor girl's arms as I flung them around my neck. I picked her up and dashed out of the apartment and down the stairs.

Standing in the alley, my heart was pounding. As someone took hold of Sylvia, my thoughts again raced to my sister on the third floor. By now, flames were blazing through the bottom floors of the house. It was only a matter of minutes before the home would be completely consumed by the fire. I ran back up the steps, but by this point the fire had spread into the staircase. I raced outside to the back of the house and stopped under the third-floor window to our apartment. I could see smoke billowing through the cracks, but no flames had yet reached where I stood. I yelled for my sister. A second later her head appeared through the opening, sheer panic across her face.

"Blair!" she yelled. "How am I supposed to get down?!"

Are you kidding me? I thought to myself. *Does she think she has options?*

I yelled back up to her, "Jump, damn it!"

"But — I just have my robe on!" she screamed back at me.

At this point I was so mad at my sister I was ready to leave her dangling out of the window.

"B.I., for God's sake — just jump!"

My sister stared at me from above. I threw my arms up toward her, earnestly beckoning for her to jump. A deafening crack thundered in the house behind her. In terror, she flung herself over the edge of the window. Fortunately, a second-floor extension jutted out beneath the window, which angled her fall toward me. Still, I really had no thought about how to catch a body falling from a roof. So, I just opened my arms wider and hoped for the best. She landed right on top of me. As we both fell to the ground, I heard B.I. groan. I looked over and she was holding her ankle pretty tight.

I knelt beside her and asked, "You okay, B.I.?"

"I think I twisted my ankle," she replied. And then a faint smile came over her face, "but I'll be fine."

By late evening, the whole upper side of Saint John was abuzz with news of the house fire in Union Alley. Fire trucks and police vehicles had surrounded the house. Even the fire chief and building inspectors arrived to the scene — which I suspect had quite a bit to do with our alley being right behind the cherished Old Opera House on Union Street. In fact, with the house completely destroyed, they soon turned their attention to keeping smoldering ashes from catching adjacent buildings on fire.

With all this excitement, it didn't take long for local reporters to start filing in, eager to capture the story for the morning paper. As they tried to get detailed accounts of what happened, a neighbour mentioned that in all the chaos I had managed to rescue three people from the fire. Before I knew it, I was surrounded by a group of reporters pressing me with questions. They were talking so quickly I hardly had time to think or know what to say.

And then one reporter blurted out a question that struck me hard. "And where will you go now?"

By this time, relatives and neighbours had begun to fill the alley. I looked past the reporters and saw their faces, overcome with shock. Fortunately, all sixteen people at home that night survived the blaze. But the children were now standing barefoot on the road, mothers holding nothing but the hands of their young ones. The men were standing forlorn, looking emptily at the smoldering house. In a matter of minutes, three families were standing in the middle of a dirt road, without a home.

NEWS OF SAINT JOHN, LANCASTER AND DISTRICT — SAINT JOHN, N. B., FRIDAY, JUNE 11, 1954 — THE BEST FEATURES EVERY DAY — PAGE 13

LAUNCH INVESTIGATION INTO UPTOWN FIRE

View Charred Ruins Of Home

30 Are Homeless After Disastrous Conflagration

Fire Chief, Building Inspector, Red Cross Officials Inspect Badly Gutted Building At Rear Of Old Opera House

Seeking To Have Falls View Park Work Started Soon

Trade Board To Ask City To Complete Arrangements Immediately

Liberal Leader Attacks Policy Of Government

A. C. Taylor Addresses St. John County Association Meeting

THE MAN on the STREET

Noted Musician Succumbs

Was One Of Adjudicators At N. B. Festival This Year

News article highlighting Blair's heroics in the tragic fire that destroyed the home of three families on Union Alley, 1954.

"I don't know," I said to the reporter, without looking at him, "we lost everything, even our clothes. I have no idea what we're going to do."

Some neighbours decided to take in the mothers and the littlest ones, while the rest began to wander over to the office of the Canadian Red Cross. My mother led the procession down Prince William Street until we stood in front of the office door. My father, as I recall, followed from a distance, barely noticeable, standing apart on the darkened streets. Apparently, word had already spread that a fire had rendered over thirty people destitute, for just moments after we arrived, a fellow came running up to greet us. I learned later it was Mr. Slader, chairman of the Red Cross disaster committee. He was already busy arranging rooms for us at a local Saint John hotel.

The next morning, Red Cross volunteers came to our hotel rooms, handing us food and clothing. During the following days they came back to make sure we had enough to get by. Apparently, the mayor went over to inspect the ruins the next day. Seeing nothing beyond our house was damaged, he said to the media still milling around that it was a "regrettable affair" — but declined to offer any further action. He remarked how fortunate it was that the Opera House had been spared of any damage, and off he went. Eventually, the families realized there was no further support coming. In the end, there was nothing left to do but go our separate ways. My folks ended up finding a small place on the east side of town. The others dispersed to different parts of the city. The families remained close, but truthfully, the fire changed everything. Life was never the same for our family as it was on Union Alley.

• • •

My father falls silent and leans back into his old armchair. I look at him in disbelief. How is this the first time ever hearing about him saving people from a burning house? I imagine the tremendous respect my father must have gained as a result of this heroic act.

"Dad, what did your father say to you after rescuing those people from the fire?"

"Nothing, really," my father replies. "Between us it was as if nothing had happened."

I'm dumbfounded. "I don't get it. That was a pretty heroic thing you did. Surely it must have changed his perception of you, changed your relationship, at least in a small way?"

A resigned look comes over my father's face. "No, and to be honest, at the time I didn't think it would matter. School made a bit of a fuss about the whole thing. The church didn't make any mention of it, which I guess disappointed me a little bit, for I spent a whole lot of time at the church. But as for my father, it never occurred to me what he thought. This may be hard to believe, but truthfully it quickly became a moment that just came and went in my life."

I am immediately reminded again of the contrast between my father's generation and mine. I just couldn't imagine my parents and siblings saying *nothing* between us if our house burned down.

Which brings me to ask, "And how about your mother? She must have spoken to you about what happened?"

"Well," my dad replies, "she was upset obviously, for a whole lot of reasons. But mostly, she was grateful. After all, there were few things in her life that were of any value, except her children. And, since the fire spared her the grief of losing any one of us, she had God to thank for that at least. And Mama knew the best response to the situation, for the sake of her family, was to take a deep breath and carry on — which is exactly what we did."

"And what did you do?" I ask.

"What else could I do?" my father responds. "I left home. With the only place I had ever lived in now gone, and the hardship of starting life again hanging over everyone, I was even more determined to set off on my own path. I'll tell you what happened next though."

• • •

Somehow, in the two weeks that followed the fire, I managed to write all my final papers and graduate from high school. A few days later I left to go work at the YMCA summer camp. In the midst of that, I went to the Canadian Olympic training program for track and field in Toronto for two weeks. That was the motivation I needed to really spread my wings. When I returned, I decided to sign up for the air force. I had spent five years in air cadets during school. My brothers had spent their school in the army cadet program. Of course, my father wanted me to be in the army, because the army is where *real* men fight with boots on the ground and look our enemy in the eye. Anyway, in November I was called to begin air force training.

At the time, I was working as a cleaner in the theatre behind our house, where they showed feature films. I would often stay behind after my shift to sneak in and watch films from the back door. On the night I was to leave for training, they were showing *Three Coins in the Fountain*, where Frank Sinatra sings the title song. Well, wouldn't you know, I lost track of time. As the credits started rolling, I raced home. I'll never forget how angry my mama was that I'd missed the dinner she made for me! I simply hugged my mother, kissed her goodbye, and ran to the train station with only a few minutes to spare and fewer dollars in my pocket.

I ended up being away for a year and one month, returning the week before Christmas. In fact, over the course of four years I would leave and only return again at Christmas. I did enjoy life in the military. At the same time, being away from home, I began to think about the best moments in life, and the people who most cared about me. I kept recalling the peace I experienced every Saturday morning in worship, and the joy of singing in the choir those many years. I really felt close to God, and the feeling of being valued by the people I served never left me. I started picturing a life of me caring for a congregation, mentoring young people in the faith, in the same way that Father Mark mentored me. At the same time, I was deeply torn, for I knew this path would only make my father even more disappointed in me. At some point I was going to have to reckon with the man. As I started to think about heading home, the dread of facing his disappointment haunted me. Even after all the military training I went through, this was a fear I was still unsure I was prepared to face.

By now, Mama and Papa had moved into an apartment for seniors in the east end of town. I got off the train at Union Station and started the long walk to see them. I still had my military boots and uniform on, and by the time I reached their walkway I was sweating and my feet were sore. What happened next I still can't believe, even though I've played it back in my mind a thousand times. My father, surprisingly, was out on the front step talking with two other men. Papa looked up to see me approach from the end of the walkway. He then straightened up, dropped his cigarette to the ground, and started walking toward me. I froze in my tracks, for I had no clue what he was going to do when he reached me. About a foot away, he stopped. He took a long, serious look at my uniform. Then, before I knew it, he pulled me close and wrapped his arms around me. Now, you think I would be relieved — but it scared the hell out of me!

Putting his hand on my shoulder, he turned me around and led me to where the other men stood watching. As we approached, my father bellowed, "I want you to meet my son! He just returned from serving in the air force!"

I stood in stunned silence. I'm not sure if I felt anger or joy — or both. As his buddies drifted away down the street, I stared intensely at my father. Before I could stop them, the words poured out of me. "You do know that's the first time you've ever called me 'son,' right?" It was more of an accusation than a question.

He froze, his hand still half-raised from waving goodbye to his friends. For a moment, he looked as though I'd struck him. His mouth opened, but nothing came out. I turned away, ready to leave him standing there.

Then I heard his voice, rough, low, almost breaking. "Blair … when I look at you now, I see a piece of me that never died. A piece I thought the war had buried. I lost my pride in how I failed so miserably at being a soldier — and ever since I been tryin' to hide my shame in what I become. I see you come down that road, and my pride came back to me, son."

I kept my back to him.

"I know I let you down, my boy. You had dreams, and I paid no attention them —"

I spun back to him, raw. "You paid no attention to *me*! Do you know what that was like? For your own father to ignore you —"

"More than you care to know!" An aching rage now rang in my father's voice. "Not once in this life was I called *son*. And not one person on this earth taught me how to be a *father* to a son. So don't start telling me about being alone in this world unless you're ready to do some hard listening yourself, son."

His face twisted with regret. "Look, if I could turn back time, Blair, I'd give you the moments I never gave you —"

I felt my chest tighten. "And what — now you think a few words can fix it?"

My father dropped his gaze to the concrete below. "You're right, no changin' the past."

For the first time in my life, I saw him not as a traumatized soldier, nor as a threatening father figure tormented by a hidden past, but simply as a man — standing there, stripped of excuses, hoping for another chance in life.

And for the first time, I wasn't afraid to be in his presence. Life never really gave my father and me the chance to rewrite what had passed between us. Before long, I left home again — this time to Detroit, where I became a pastor with a congregation of my own. But as I was finding my voice in the pulpit, his health began to falter. He had always intended to work until the day he died, but the drinking had taken its toll. Then came the accident on the construction site. He lost several fingers, and after that, he could never work again. The bottle claimed more and more of him, and eventually diabetes set in, stripping his body one limb at a time. I will never forget the day I got the call from back home: The doctors said they needed to amputate his leg.

• • •

My father glances over at me. "I took you to see him."

I nod. "Yes, I remember that. It was hard standing by his bed. He looked so frail — not the man I remembered as a child."

"No," my father responds. "Not nearly the man he was. But I was afraid that might be the last chance for you to share words with him.... Turned out it was."

I never forgot the moment of standing at my grandfather's bedside. For the longest time, I kept a photo that the nurse took of us. Somehow, I lost it while moving to Alberta — how I wish I still had that last image I ever saw of him. The words of George wash up from the shores of that distant memory, and I find myself echoing them: "I made you carry my burdens. Don't carry them anymore ..."

At the time, I didn't really appreciate what Papa was saying. But now, after learning about the life they shared together, I understood.

"That was the last we spoke," my father whispers. "A few months later, on February 2, 1980, my father left this earth. My mother — who had spent a lifetime praying for him, carrying her own share of his struggles — followed just weeks later. It was as though, with him gone, her work was finished."

I was ten years old when Papa died. Most of my aunts and uncles were not the religious type, and they were quite happy, relieved in fact, to leave all the funeral arrangements to my father. But when everyone had assembled and the time came for my father to lead the service, every soul was singing, every foot moving, and every hand clapping to the cadence of my father's preaching. It was another palpable moment I recall as a child, of sitting beneath the pulpit when my father preached, and feeling a sense of pride. But never did I feel such strength of pride as I did on that day when my father inspired all of us as he commended Papa's soul to his eternal rest.

As the last remnants of family and friends began drifting from the hall, my mom sent me to tell Dad we were ready to go. I found him in the pastor's office, sitting in the dark with his back to the door, staring out the window into the night sky.

"Dad," I whispered. "Mom says we're ready to go."

George and Muriel Dixon on their fiftieth wedding anniversary.

Instinctively, he turned his head, and as he did the tears on his face were captured by the slim rays of moonlight. He wiped them away quickly as he turned his face back to the window. "Okay, son," he said. "Tell your mom I'll be there in a minute."

I never forgot that moment. It was the first time I had ever seen him cry. I would not see that same depth of grief on my father's face again for another forty years — the day we stood together once again to remember his father.

10

One Hundred Years

Ours is not the struggle of one day, one week, or one year.
Ours is not the struggle of one judicial appointment or presidential term.
Ours is the struggle of a lifetime, or maybe even many lifetimes, and each one of us in every generation must do our part.

—JOHN LEWIS, U.S. Congress member and civil rights activist

A few days after leaving my father and returning to Calgary, I receive a call from him. He says that an advisory committee is being set up by the Department of

National Defence for the planning of the national apology next summer. As one of the oldest living descendants, they want my father on the committee. My father agreed, but on the condition that I join him.

Our first meeting is with Russell Grosse, the co-chair of the committee. Russell works full-time as the director of the Black Cultural Centre for Nova Scotia, and he's been a leading advocate in the movement for a formal apology to be offered to descendants of the Black Battalion. Russell explains that the streamed sessions would be in the form of town hall meetings, with the intent to hear from descendants and distinguished members of the Black community about their expectations for such an apology to be made.

A few weeks later, I am back in Regina with my dad and sitting in his living room with my laptop open to the online session. Russell Grosse begins with a humble recognition of the long years it took for us to arrive at this point in history. He emphasizes its value for our Black communities, and his hope for the healing that would follow. He then invites us to move into virtual breakout groups and provide input on a series of questions related to the national apology event. This first round seems productive. At the very least, it provides a long overdue forum for descendants from across the country to connect. We spend much of the time sharing our collective experiences of the impact generations of discrimination has had upon our communities. Russell announces there will be more virtual gatherings to follow. My father and I leave the session feeling hopeful.

As the sessions move through the winter months, however, the tone of the meetings starts to change. Increasingly, lower-level military officials dominate the discussion. The same questions start being repeated from previous sessions, with not much indication of the agenda moving into preparing for the event. I begin to wonder what our actual role is in the whole process. When I raise this issue, they assure me our input is being taken into consideration. With these words, the proceedings carry on.

Around Easter, they announce a break in the meeting schedule. By the time we reconvene, we are only weeks away from the date the apology is to take place. Heading into the meeting, I can feel myself shift from anxiety to frustration for not having been given answers already. During one of the first town hall meetings, I make the point that travel and accommodation should not be the responsibility of the direct descendants. After all, many are pensioners scattered in the far reaches of the country. And now, as we begin the last scheduled meeting before the event, none of the descendants has yet received any word about the government's plans to get us there.

The session begins with military officials reporting details about parade routes, reception locations, meal menus, VIP accommodations, and their itineraries. I interrupt them.

"Sorry, this sounds like a wonderful event you are planning, which I am sure descendants would love to attend, but at this point no word has been mentioned at all regarding their travel and accommodation. So, what arrangements have you made?"

There is a moment of silence across the virtual screens. Then, a woman who had earlier introduced herself as a secretary for the defence department opens her mic. The look on her face seems to suggest she is perplexed, as if she doesn't understand the point of my question.

"Well …" she replies, "you are on your own to get here and find a place to stay. Maybe check with the Truro tourist site. Or you could watch it online, I think plans are underway to have it streamed …"

I watch her lips continue to move, but my thoughts drown out the sound of her voice. She basically confirmed what I had come to fear. This was turning out to be simply another performative event on the part of the government. This time, it would be my grandfather flashed on a brochure or an Instagram post to demonstrate how "tolerant" our nation is. Within circles of social activists, there is a running joke that Prime Minister Trudeau has handed out more apologies than Christmas cards. It's the kind of public spectacle that draws international attention, and makes the average, well-intentioned voter feel a little more comfortable about being Canadian. After all, it's nice to be regarded as a progressive nation on the world stage.

We commit the moral felony too often, people in power obscuring justice through self-aggrandizing acts of charity. We feel good about giving out of our abundance, and care little about the extent to which the condition of those oppressed has changed. Let's be honest: Comfort is addictive. And participating in real justice is anything but comfortable. It requires some kind of permanent shift in our position of privilege to bring fairness to a situation. Obscuring acts of justice with words of contrition is really just a form of self-preservation. Moreover, in this case, the government telling the descendants they need to pay their own way to receive an apology for the injustice inflicted against them — that is the definition of moral hypocrisy. I have to confess, it takes everything in me not to lose my temper in the middle of that meeting. But as the last people leave the meeting, I can no longer hold it in.

While my father and I commiserate in his living room, we're left a little uncertain where to go with our grievances. As a whole, despite their good intentions, the planning committee were clearly not grasping the bigger picture of what was happening. However, there is one person who had been occasionally involved in the meetings who I believe will appreciate our concern. His name is Douglas Ruck — the son of the late Senator Calvin Ruck. Douglas had followed in his father's footsteps as a civil rights activist, as well as being a lawyer in Nova Scotia. I know he will offer wisdom on the concerns my father and I are wrestling with. And if he agrees, I'm hoping a man of his reputation might get them to listen to what we have to say. My dad agrees.

Two days after discussing this issue with Douglas Ruck, I receive an email from Russell Grosse. He asks if my father and I would be willing to further discuss our concerns with him and Lt. Col. Barry Pitcher, the co-chair of the national advisory committee. In the meantime, he assures me that my concerns will be formally included in the official records that are being submitted to the Canadian government in the coming weeks. A few days later we are able to meet online. Dad and I begin by expressing our deep appreciation for their dedication to making this moment possible, and we emphasize our view that their own intentions are not the issue, but more with how the process seems to be unfolding. They acknowledge important things are being overlooked and will make sure these issues are corrected before the event takes place. Two days later, I receive a phone call from the executive assistant to Anita Anand, the minister of defence. He wants me to know that Minister Anand had received word of our concerns and would address them directly with the committee.

It turns out, though, my voice is not the only one getting her attention. I had been keeping my sister and brother up to date on what was happening. Lisa, my sister, is the owner of a very popular café in downtown Peterborough, where many faculty of Trent University often gather. It happened that Minister Anand was visiting the campus and a faculty member invited her to join them for dessert at Lisa's café. My sister, herself a fierce advocate for marginalized voices in her community, did not miss the opportunity to convey our family's frustrations over a complimentary dessert.

And, in fairness, Minister Anand was deeply sympathetic to our cause. She herself shares lived experience of growing up as a racialized person in eastern Canada. Given her personal interest in greater inclusion, she was public in her commitment to foster greater diversity in the nation's military institutions. This issue our family faced was simply another reminder that real systemic change is a generational journey, which doesn't finish simply by putting a person of colour behind a desk. Elected officials don't last very long — enduring change happens when the *cultures* of our institutions change.

Soon after our interactions with the minister of defence, we get word from Russell Grosse that a retired captain by the name of Kevin Junor is being appointed to coordinate the remainder of the planning process. As a Black man who spent his whole career in the military, he had to overcome prejudice while proving himself over many missions as a capable soldier. He understands the perspective of the families, as well as the mindset of military personnel. I feel privileged getting to know Captain Junor fairly well in these weeks. Under his leadership, things seem to finally come together.

I get a call that the government is committed to paying the costs for direct descendants to witness the apology in person. Finally, I feel we are truly ready for the moment.

On the morning of July 9, 2022, I stand in front of my father in our room on the second floor of the Inn on Prince Hotel & Conference Centre in Truro, helping him with the final details of his attire. As I gently wrap the tie around his neck, I am struck by this rare moment of intimacy between us. Holding up his old military blazer, my father shifts his frail shoulders as he tries to fit into it. It took a lot for my father to travel to this event. And since arriving it's been a whirlwind of functions across Nova Scotia. We travelled by bus to see the Black Battalion monument in Pictou, sat in hotel reception halls with military brass, and drove in an escorted convoy to the town of Cherry Brook for a banquet at the Black Cultural Centre hosted by the premier of Nova Scotia. This morning, I can feel the weight of my father's fatigue as he leans on my arm. But as I push the last buttons through his shirt and trousers, the anticipation seems to breathe fresh energy into him. In his mind, I am sure there is nothing that will keep him from witnessing the moment to come.

I take a step back.

"Well, Dad," I say. "You look ready to take on the world."

"Let's go then, son." And with that, we set off down to the lobby.

Descendants at the No. 2 monument in Pictou, Nova Scotia, with the current mayor of the village Supt, in eastern France, closest to where the No. 2 Battalion was stationed.

Under the watchful eye of Captain Junor, military officials hastily escort descendants and distinguished guests into chauffeured vehicles. The streets are eerily silent as our procession winds its way to the grounds of the cricket field outside the Truro golf course, where the soldiers of the Black Battalion had once assembled for their training a little over a hundred years before. Security is tight, as would be expected for the arrival of the prime minister. Even inside the vehicles, both officials and guests quietly look out the windows. The sight of abandoned streets creates an air of anxiety about how the event will unfold.

As we approach the grounds, however, all that uncertainty quickly disappears. The scene emerges before us beneath a brilliant blue sky. Hundreds of people are streaming into the stands erected just for the occasion. Marching bands are striking up tunes while soldiers proudly parade along the green fields in uniforms from various units that span generations. Both old and young seem equally excited to be part of this historic occasion. Early on in this endeavour, I was doubtful whether this moment would be shared by much more than the handful of descendants. But now I can see, no I can actually *feel*, that this moment is going to belong to all of us.

As the formal ceremony finally gets under way, there is the usual line of officials to the podium, each offering their own

Blair receiving a commemorative medal of honour for soldiers of the No. 2 Battalion from then-Defence Minister Anita Anand, with National Apology Advisory Committee co-chairs Lt. Col. Barry Pitcher (*left*) and Russell Grosse (*right*).

version of what this day means for them and their constituents. They all offer commitments to not see the injustices of the past repeated on their watch. However, as Senator Wanda Thomas Bernard stands before the podium, something feels different. Dr. Bernard is the first Black Nova Scotian to hold a tenure-track position at Dalhousie University. As a social worker and educator, Bernard has worked tirelessly to promote mental health in rural Black communities and to teach new Black Canadians about legislative rights for citizen engagement. If there is a voice that understands the significance of this moment for our generation, it is Senator Bernard. There is a palpable hush in the audience as she begins to speak:

> I want you to imagine what life was like for African Nova Scotians in 1915. Anti-Black racism was flourishing here in Nova Scotia, across this country — as it is today. Yes, slavery had been abolished, but anti-Black racism took root. Life on the margins, harsh conditions, inadequate means to provide for their families. Yet they made a way, out of no way. Our ancestors were survivors! And they were loyal Canadians, even though, even though they had a lifetime of second-class citizenship in this country. Imagine, imagine. Despite their personal,

> family and community struggles, they were also concerned about the global war effort, the First World War. Imagine they wanted to help. But they were denied the right to fight for their country. Imagine, they had to fight their country — to fight for their country! To fight for our country! To have the right to join the global war effort. Hence, the No. 2 Construction Battalion was formed. Imagine the sacrifice and dedication. Imagine the fear and determination. Imagine the willingness to put your country first — even when that country didn't value or respect you.

People's spirits are stirring from her prophetic reminder of what our ancestors endured. In that moment I can't help but ponder the reason for such endurance. How have people of the African diaspora transcended such great oppression over the last five hundred years? At every turn, beaten down to the point of being extinguished from history, they have found the capacity to dig deep and persevere. If you ask the ancestors, they will tell you our people thrive because our spiritual roots run deep. Physical adversity cannot impoverish the souls of people who pray. It was Black American writer and civil rights activist Maya Angelou who said it best, that despite every effort to diminish the soul of Black folk in the desert of oppression, *still we rise.* And now, gathered in the heat of the sun, on the very ground where our ancestors trained for battle, descendants embody the hope of a generation past. Our hearts are ready, and the anticipation is mounting. When Prime Minister Justin Trudeau at last is led to the podium, there is a swell of excitement in the audience. And then, with a hundred years pressing into one historic moment, we wait for the words to usher forth:*

> When the First World War broke out in Europe and Canada joined the fight, men from across the country flocked to enlist. Among those brave volunteers were hundreds of young Black men …
>
> In repeated acts of discrimination and racism, almost every single Black volunteer was turned away and denied the honour of serving their country.... [R]ecruiters did not see men willing to fight for our collective freedom. They only saw the colour of their skin.... This is what systemic racism and anti-Black hate does.

---

* For a transcript of Trudeau's apology, see pm.gc.ca/en/news/speeches/2022/07/09/prime-ministers-remarks-apologize-descendants-no-2-construction-battalion.

As he delivers this final note, Prime Minister Trudeau's voice rises. A collective "Amen!" fills the air. Voices become shrill with spiritual fervour. There is nothing to hold back history now. We're in the moment. Never before had words about the Black struggle in this nation been articulated so clearly by one holding the power of government. People are rising from their chairs, urging the prime minister on through shouts and ululations. Sitting under the canopy, just rows behind my father, I bow my head in solemn prayer as I wait for the one word we all came to hear.

"As a country, we failed to recognize their contributions ... We owe these men, these brave Black men, so much. I am here today to offer the Government of Canada's official apology for the appalling way these patriots were treated."

By now, applause is thundering through the makeshift arena. With my head still bowed, I can feel the bodies all around me rising from their chairs.

"For the overt racism of turning Black volunteers away when they offered to sacrifice their lives for all — we are sorry. For not letting Black service members fight alongside their white compatriots, for denying members of No. 2 Construction Battalion the care and support they deserved — we are sorry."

By now, I can hardly hear the prime minister over the celebration erupting all around me.

Blair and Lance preparing to hear the formal apology from Prime Minister Trudeau.

"For failing to honour and commemorate the contributions of the members of the No. 2 Construction Battalion and their descendants, for the blatant anti-Black hate and systemic racism that denied these men dignity in life and in death — we are sorry."

Again, whistles and shouts fill the air. I can feel the tremor of a thousand feet tapping the earth. I lift my head and look around. Strangers and uniformed soldiers are hugging each other. As I peer at the front, I can see that my father has somehow managed to get out of his chair. Despite his frail legs, he stands tall and stoic. His eyes are covered by his dark glasses, but I am close enough to see tears beneath them. In my heart, there is no doubt what this moment means to him.

And then, thanking one last time the organizers who persevered in making this moment happen, the prime minister leaves the stage to another round of applause.

Before returning to his chair, however, Prime Minister Trudeau pauses in front of my father, who happens to be seated right next to the stage. I can see the prime minister reaching for my father's hand. And then, he bows his head so close that their foreheads are nearly touching. As they stand together, I can see the lips of the prime minister move as he utters the words, "I'm sorry."

My father, in turn, simply nods his head. As the prime minister takes his leave, I can see my father's shoulders rise, as if the weight of a hundred years had finally been lifted.

• • •

A few weeks after the national apology event, I receive a call from the producers of *W5*, the Canadian television documentary program. The poignant moment between my father and the prime minister of Canada had been captured on television. The producer tells me that Sandie Rinaldo, the host of the show, wants an interview with us, to hear our thoughts about that historic day. If we agree, she can fly out west to meet us the following week.

It's a beautiful mid-afternoon in early September 2022. Sandie Rinaldo makes herself comfortable in the same living room where I spent many hours listening to my father share the story of his life, his father, and the legacy of the war. As he recounts all that transpired, and the way he was personally impacted by the formal apology that took place some weeks earlier, Sandie Rinaldo leans in and asks him, "As your father's representative today, do you think he would accept that apology and say, yes that's good enough for me?"

My dad looks intently at Sandie. "My father had a tough life. It was tough when I was young, but I grew out of that. Papa — he didn't have a chance to grow out of that. If they at that time, with my father and those guys, if they said, 'We're

Blair receiving an apology from Prime Minister Trudeau during the ceremony, July 9, 2022.

going to do something about this,' my father would have simply said, 'Well *hallelujah*.'"

At this moment, the reality that George Dixon was never afforded a word of dignity or redemption in his lifetime finally, it seems, sinks in for my father. He shifts awkwardly in his seat. As he continues to speak, tears fill his eyes: "But for me, to speak for my father now, I won't even try. I won't even try."

CONCLUSION

A Future for My People

Don't let anybody, anybody convince you
this is the way the world is and therefore
must be. It must be the way it ought to be.

—TONI MORRISON, Sarah Lawrence
College commencement speech, 1998

Anyone who teaches high school students today is constantly reminded that teenagers don't really care how much you know, until they know how much you care. Here's something else I've come to recognize — that's true regardless of their racial or cultural background. Having a sense of belonging is essential for human flourishing. We witness that time and again among those who feel vulnerable and powerless, like teenagers feeling stuck in schools where they are constantly being evaluated, or people of colour who have nowhere to hide from the unpredictable violence of racism. If trauma is passed on through generations, then we can't assume all people feel the same sense of belonging in the places we occupy. We need to make a point of expressing genuine love and gratitude for one another, especially to those we suspect may have not heard those words spoken to them in the past.

In my work promoting racial equity in our school communities, I have come to appreciate the very real impact generational trauma has on people. There is an author named Resmaa Menakem who is a therapist and social worker in the Minneapolis neighbourhood where George Floyd was murdered at the hands of police officers on that fateful day of May 25, 2020. As the global media zeroed in on this incident that had suddenly ignited fury and protests across the world, the work of Resmaa Menakem quickly came to light. A couple of years before the George Floyd tragedy, he had written a powerful book entitled *My Grandmother's Hands*. He used that image as a way of describing how trauma seeps into our flesh and bones, and manifests in our bodies like a memory haunting our nerves and senses. In his book, Menakem speaks about the psychological impact white supremacy has had on people living in bodies with different skin. He contends that the pathway to mending our hearts is to change the way we relate to our bodies. This act of redefining the narrative around the melatonin in our skin, Menakem argues, is deeply empowering. He goes on to explore how this internal empowerment ripples outward from one body to another, and from groups of bodies into our systems and structures, to eventually transform the very societies in which we live.

As I reread this collective memoir my father and I wrote back in the summer of 2022 about my grandfather's life and legacy, I am deeply moved by those in his story who tried to offer him compassion and hope in the moments he felt most alienated. In particular, I keep going back to Cassie Maxwell. More than anyone, Cassie stood by my grandfather, sacrificed much, and even risked her own name so that he, in turn, might make a name for himself. I've realized my family owes a lot of gratitude for the way Cassie cared for our papa, especially during a time when her own life was hard. We should, in some way, honour the women who did as much for our community as the men who fought overseas.

At first, though, I wasn't sure how to go about it. After all, it was impossible to express that gratitude to Cassie herself. And, unfortunately, the only record I could find of Cassie's descendants was a great-grandson who died relatively early in life in the midst of a military career. The obituary mentioned he had one son who survived him, but I couldn't find any trace of how to contact him. I checked the funeral home website where Cassie's great-grandson had been buried. I found a tribute page still posted there, along with an email to send words of condolence to surviving family members. Given how many years had passed, I wondered if someone was checking this email, or if it was even active. But, as Menakem pointed out, every redemptive word is like a small ripple that brings healing into the world. Perhaps there was a person still connected to that email. Perhaps a word of appreciation could contribute, even in a small way, to a sense of pride in their own story. Were they aware of the impact she had made on this one person's life? I decided I would send my message of gratitude.

After introducing myself, I spoke about the relationship between Cassie and my grandfather George and how she became a mother to him during his teenage years. When the First World War broke out, I recalled how Cassie signed George's military papers as his "next of kin." This enabled my grandfather to join the only Black battalion ever assembled in Canadian history. I acknowledged that we often speak of the men of the Battalion but neglect to hold up the women who also sacrificed so much in support of the effort. I concluded by expressing my desire for them, as descendants, to know our gratitude for Cassie's love of our papa, George Dixon. Their ancestor gave our ancestor a precious gift — a belief he had purpose in life.

I'm not sure if anyone received my email. One day, I hope I may learn that someone did. Since sending that email, I've been thinking a lot about all the negative messaging on social media these days. While mostly festering in echo chambers, we see politicians amplifying these narratives, distorting truth with hateful and fear-mongering rhetoric that galvanizes their base. In effect, we learn to mistrust one another and lose faith in working toward a greater common good. Ultimately, I believe social division is fundamentally fuelled by greed. We want more from this world than we actually deserve. We exploit the weak and diminish their humanity in order to justify our actions. From the beginning, racism has always been a means to justify the obscene greed of nations for more land and cheap labour. And still today the privileged class continues to perpetuate this narrative for power and profit. They may cloak the agenda in different forms, but the objective is the same.

At the same time, facing the outcome of a world driven by such greed on an apocalyptic scale, youth are demonstrating remarkable courage in voicing a new vision for the future. They are fighting fear and anxiety with a resilient hope. One day I got a call from my eldest niece, Jade, who had recently been hired as a teacher in a school just outside of Toronto.

"I've been asked to do a student presentation about our ancestor George Dixon during Black History month," she explained quite excitedly. "They asked me to connect his story to the theme of 'joy in the outdoors.' I have an idea I want to run by you."

Okay, I thought, this I will need to hear. To be honest, I was grasping for any connection between "joy in the outdoors" and what I had spent the previous months learning about my grandfather! But, as someone who hangs around young people for a living, I am constantly reminded that they possess something my generation has largely lost — perspective.

After we exchanged different ideas, I truly believed she had come up with an inspiring message for the students. When it came time for her presentation, my niece began by reflecting on the countless forests and rivers that sustained our ancestors as they escaped from slavery along the underground railroad. Despite the hardship of navigating the wilderness, the "outdoors" was one place they felt free from oppression. My niece then shared the moments when Papa, when he was still young, fled across open waters in search of his own freedom.

"It seems as though adventure," my niece suggested to the students, "was a way for him to escape the all too familiar climate of racism that Black Canadians faced every day. I believe the ocean and the great outdoors was a place to find salvation, and gave him critical hope for the future."

Jade was also in attendance on that historic day in Nova Scotia, when the national apology was given. She shared with students the inspiring message of Senator Wanda Bernard, urging us to continue to imagine — in light of the cost others paid for our freedom. My niece then leaned closer to the mic and placed this thought before the young audience:

> Imagine. For my great-grandfather, he didn't have the privilege of imagining. He lived it. Throughout your life I encourage you to keep imagining what life is like to walk through this world as a person of colour. I want to invite you to imagine what life was like for my great-grandfather, those he fought with, what they truly fought for, and the cost each of them paid to live in a world where every human could perhaps one day be free. But most importantly, keep this in mind. Imagining leads to empathy, empathy leads to action, and it is action that leads to change.

And bringing her hand over her heart, she closed by saying, "The future begins here."

As I look back on the historic day of the formal apology, I realize that moment was more about vindication than honour. After all, my grandfather, a soldier of the segregated No. 2 Construction Battalion, a labourer, a father, and a man burdened by hard living, never received parades or medals in his lifetime. He was afforded no dignity by the privileged in society whom he risked his life to protect. In the end, he died penniless. And yet, I am also persuaded to believe there is something poignant about the title Anthony Sherwood chose for his documentary about the men of the Black Battalion, *Honour Before Glory.* It is true, their honour was not found in the glory of battle, or from decorated medals of valour, or stone monuments on which their names would outlive generations. In the months of listening to his stories, however, I learned what kind of man my grandfather truly was.

Yes, my grandfather struggled with a deeply broken spirit through much of his life. But in his youth, he stood

Commemorative plaque of Private George Dixon (Jennifer Dow, artist).

courageously for loyalty, and in his dying days he once again revealed the true depth of his courage — by choosing forgiveness. I believe, looking down from that street corner in heaven, his shiny cornet resting in his hands as he watches his family return home from his own funeral, he would have felt most honoured in the silence of that darkened church office, in the tears of his son who mourned for him. I believe George Dixon feels honoured that, through his hardships, his grandson is learning a vital lesson — the true weight of redemption my ancestors carried. I believe he feels honoured that his great-granddaughter saw salvation in his struggle and has hope for the future because he showed us that our inner light is never truly extinguished, no matter how dark our days become. This, I believe, is how George Dixon is honoured without receiving any worldly glory. This is what I believe will forever remain his legacy.

ACKNOWLEDGEMENTS

It simply would not have been possible to complete this written portrait of my grandfather without the valuable and timely contribution of others. I am indebted to Allen Grant, who brought to light George Dixon's military files. I am grateful to Jennifer McInerney-Dow for her dedication to the history of the No. 2 Battalion, and for revealing the crucial whereabouts of George after leaving Africville. And I am so deeply humbled by the enthusiastic research my colleague Jennifer Perry contributed to this story. It is a result of her work, along with my other colleague Anna MacEachern, that the legacy of the No. 2 Construction Battalion will be taught in classrooms across our city.

Speaking of colleagues, my Racial JEDI (justice, equity, diversity, and inclusion) team in the Calgary Catholic School District — Nothando, Eloida, Matt, and Holly — have been unequivocal in supporting me throughout this project, and along the way have embraced my family as their own. I am grateful to Anthony Sherwood, who over the last few years has been a tremendous influence in shaping my voice as a storyteller. Likewise, I want to give a huge shout-out to my brother, Beau, who pushed my creative writing skills as we ventured to adapt the book manuscript into a musical.

To Carol Hollywood, who disregarded my claim to be an accidental author and encouraged me to submit the manuscript to a book publisher. Which leads me to acknowledging Meghan Macdonald and the team at Dundurn Press, for believing in this story! And to Carrie Gleason, my editor, for her critical research that enriched the story, along with incisive comments that enriched me as a writer.

Finally, to those who fiercely advocated for the delivery of a formal apology to the descendants of the Black Battalion soldiers, once again I express my deepest gratitude. Your fortitude inspired me to write this story, for without knowing its beginning, I was certain it would end in hope.

IMAGE CREDITS

9 Tony Spina, *Detroit Free Press*

23 The Timothy Drescher Community Murals Collection (Mark Rogovin)

31 Bob Brooks Nova Scotia Archives 1989-468 vol. 16/negative sheet 18 image 37

32 Bob Brooks Nova Scotia Archives 1989-468 vol. 16/negative sheet 6 image 11

44 Bob Brooks Nova Scotia Archives 1989-468 vol. 16/negative sheet 5 image 16

55 © Detroit Publishing Co.

74 Provincial Archives of New Brunswick

84 Jennifer Dow

89 Esther Clark Wright Archives at Acadia University/1900 .237-WWI/31

107 Museum Windsor/P6110

119 Militarybadgecollection.com

155 New Brunswick Publishing Co. Ltd.

181 (*left & right*) Courtesy CTV News *W5*

183 Courtesy CTV News *W5*

192 Jennifer Dow

ABOUT THE AUTHOR

Photo by Sergei Belski

LANCE B. DIXON currently serves as an education specialist in racial equity for the publicly funded Catholic school board in Calgary. Raised as a child of mixed-racial heritage in central Detroit during the early '70s, he is deeply conscious of the impact racism has on the formation of identity. For the past twenty-five years, he has focused on enabling organizations to foster greater inclusion through prejudice-reduction and diversity-building initiatives. Lance has completed graduate studies in theology and education and a doctoral degree in organizational leadership. His journey to finding paths of racial reconciliation has taken him to South Africa and to communities across North America. *A Footnote to Freedom* is his first book — it has been adapted by Lance and his brother, Beau Dixon, into a musical.